38.45

P9-CSB-023

363,46
Teen

TEEN RIGHTS AND FREEDOMS

I Abortion

TEEN RIGHTS AND FREEDOMS

I Abortion

Noël Merino
Book Editor

GREENHAVEN PRESS
A part of Gale, Cengage Learning

GALE
CENGAGE Learning·

Detroit • New York • San Francisco • New Haven, Conn • Waterville, Maine • London

LIBRARY OF CONGRESS CATALOGING-IN-PUBLICATION DATA

Abortion / Noël Merino, book editor.
    p. cm. -- (Teen rights and freedoms)
    Includes bibliographical references and index.
    ISBN 978-0-7377-6397-3 (hardcover)
    1. Abortion--Law and legislation--United States. I. Merino, Noël.
    KF3771.A929 2012
    342.7308'4--dc23

                                                              2012024247

Printed in the United States of America
1 2 3 4 5 6 7 16 15 14 13 12

Contents

The US Supreme Court holds in 1976 that a law requiring parental or spousal consent for abortion without any exceptions violates the rights of women.

A pro-choice organization argues that parental involvement laws—requiring either parental notice or parental consent—endanger minors seeking abortion.

Foreword

> *"In the truest sense freedom cannot be
> bestowed, it must be achieved."*
> Franklin D. Roosevelt,
> September 16, 1936

The notion of children and teens having rights is a relatively recent development. Early in American history, the head of the household—nearly always the father—exercised complete control over the children in the family. Children were legally considered to be the property of their parents. Over time, this view changed, as society began to acknowledge that children have rights independent of their parents, and that the law should protect young people from exploitation. By the early twentieth century, more and more social reformers focused on the welfare of children, and over the ensuing decades advocates worked to protect them from harm in the workplace, to secure public education for all, and to guarantee fair treatment for youths in the criminal justice system. Throughout the twentieth century, rights for children and teens—and restrictions on those rights—were established by Congress and reinforced by the courts. Today's courts are still defining and clarifying the rights and freedoms of young people, sometimes expanding those rights and sometimes limiting them. Some teen rights are outside the scope of public law and remain in the realm of the family, while still others are determined by school policies.

Each volume in the Teen Rights and Freedoms series focuses on a different right or freedom and offers an anthology of key essays and articles on that right or freedom and the responsibilities that come with it. Material within each volume is drawn from a diverse selection of primary and secondary sources—journals, magazines, newspapers, nonfiction books, organization newsletters, position papers, speeches, and government documents, with a particular emphasis on Supreme Court and lower court decisions. Volumes also include first-person narratives from young people and others involved in teen rights issues, such as parents and educators. The material is selected and arranged to highlight all the major social and legal controversies relating to the right or freedom under discussion. Each selection is preceded by an introduction that provides context and background. In many cases, the essays point to the difference between adult and teen rights, and why this difference exists.

Many of the volumes cover rights guaranteed under the Bill of Rights and how these rights are interpreted and protected in regard to children and teens, including freedom of speech, freedom of the press, due process, and religious rights. The scope of the series also encompasses rights or freedoms, whether real or perceived, relating to the school environment, such as electronic devices, dress, Internet policies, and privacy. Some volumes focus on the home environment, including topics such as parental control and sexuality.

Numerous features are included in each volume of Teen Rights and Freedoms:

- An annotated **table of contents** provides a brief summary of each essay in the volume and highlights court decisions and personal narratives.
- An **introduction** specific to the volume topic gives context for the right or freedom and its impact on daily life.
- A brief **chronology** offers important dates associated with the right or freedom, including landmark court cases.
- **Primary sources**—including personal narratives and court decisions—are among the varied selections in the anthology.
- **Illustrations**—including photographs, charts, graphs, tables, statistics, and maps—are closely tied to the text and chosen to help readers understand key points or concepts.

- An annotated list of **organizations to contact** presents sources of additional information on the topic.
- A **for further reading** section offers a bibliography of books, periodical articles, and Internet sources for further research.
- A comprehensive subject **index** provides access to key people, places, events, and subjects cited in the text.

Each volume of Teen Rights and Freedoms delves deeply into the issues most relevant to the lives of teens: their own rights, freedoms, and responsibilities. With the help of this series, students and other readers can explore from many angles the evolution and current expression of rights both historic and contemporary.

Introduction

The right to abortion established by *Roe v. Wade* (1973) is arguably the most controversial US Supreme Court decision to date. Prior to 1973, many states had laws that criminalized abortion, and states that allowed abortion usually allowed it only in limited cases. The court in *Roe* determined that the US Constitution guarantees a right to privacy and this right to privacy protects a woman's right to abortion up to the point of fetal viability. Over time, the court has made it clear that the right to abortion also extends to minors. The court has recognized that children under the age of eighteen have different rights under the law than adults. Thus, the court has identified ways in which states may place restrictions on abortion for minors that would not be required for adult women.

The constitutional right to privacy was first explicitly identified by the US Supreme Court in *Griswold v. Connecticut* (1965). In *Griswold* the court said that states may not ban the sale of contraceptives—or birth control—to married couples, arguing that there is an implicit right to marital privacy constitutionally guaranteed under the Bill of Rights. A few years later, in *Eisenstadt v. Baird* (1972), the court determined that the right to privacy regarding contraceptives also extends to unmarried people. These cases laid the framework for the court's reasoning on abortion in 1973.

The right to privacy was vital to the US Supreme Court's landmark ruling in *Roe*, establishing a woman's right to abortion. Justice Harry Blackmun, who authored the court's opinion in *Roe*, noted, "This right of privacy . . . is broad enough to encompass a woman's decision whether or not to terminate her pregnancy." The right to abortion is not absolute, however, and the court recognized that some state regulation was allowed: "We . . . conclude that the right of personal privacy includes the abortion decision, but that this right is not unqualified, and must be considered against important state interests in regulation." Thus, the court allowed states to regulate abortion as they regulate other medical procedures, in order to protect the health of the pregnant woman. Additionally, the court determined that the state's interest in protecting fetal life was not relevant until the third trimester, at which point the states could disallow abortion "except when it is necessary to preserve the life or health of the mother."

Just a few years after the *Roe* decision, in *Planned Parenthood of Central Missouri v. Danforth* (1976), the US Supreme Court struck down a state law that required parental consent—without any exceptions—in order for a minor to obtain an abortion. The court then extended the right to contraceptives to minors in *Carey v. Population Services International* (1977), reasoning that state laws banning the sale of contraceptive devices to minors violate their right to privacy. The court later determined, however, that states may require parental involvement for a minor's abortion if there is an alternative procedure available for a minor to get permission without the involvement of parents. In *Bellotti v. Baird* (1979), the court held that a parental-consent restriction on minors' abortions is constitutional as long as there is an option for the minor to obtain permission from a court through a judicial bypass alternative.

The above US Supreme Court decisions illustrate how teenagers' right to abortion is protected and how it is different from adults. At the core of the difference between a teenager's right to abortion and an adult woman's right to abortion is the fact that minors are under the care of parents or those acting as parents. Because of this, the court has allowed states to enact restrictions that limit the abortion rights of teenagers by imposing parental involvement requirements. Nonetheless, the court has noted that the privacy rights of teenagers are strong enough to necessitate an alternative to parental involvement, mandating that states with parental consent or parental notification laws must allow pregnant minors the ability to gain consent for abortion through a judicial process.

Almost four decades after *Roe* established the constitutional right to abortion, the issue remains contentious. There are those who believe the US Supreme Court erred in establishing a right to abortion, those who believe the decision in *Roe* was the right one, and those who believe that the court has allowed too many restrictions on abortion. Teenage abortion is particularly controversial and competing opinions abound on the issue of parental involvement restrictions. The authors in *Teen Rights and Freedoms: Abortion* explore the major court decisions involving abortion and the public debates about the abortion rights of women and teenagers.

Chronology

1965   In *Griswold v. Connecticut* the US Supreme Court first recognizes freedom of intimate association, which it said guarantees a right to privacy for married couples, finding a state law prohibiting the use of contraceptives unconstitutional.

1972   In *Eisenstadt v. Baird* the US Supreme Court rules that the right to privacy protects the right of unmarried couples to use birth control.

1973   In *Roe v. Wade* the US Supreme Court determines that the right to privacy protects the right of women to choose abortion in the early stages of pregnancy.

1976   In *Planned Parenthood of Central Missouri v. Danforth* the US Supreme Court holds that states may not require parental consent for a minor's abortion without any exceptions, striking down one of many abortion restrictions implemented by Missouri.

1977   In *Carey v. Population Services International* the US Supreme Court rules that the rights to privacy and intimate association identified in *Griswold v. Connecticut* (1965) also

extend to minors, protecting their right
to access contraceptives.

1979　　In *Bellotti v. Baird* the US Supreme
Court rules that parental consent for
a minor's abortion can be required as
long as there is the alternative for a
judicial bypass granting permission.

1980　　In *Harris v. McRae* the US Supreme
Court holds that it is constitutional for
federal funding of abortion through
Medicaid to be restricted and that
states participating in Medicaid are not
required to fund medically necessary
abortions.

1983　　In *Akron v. Akron Center for Reproductive Health, Inc.* the US Supreme
Court determines, among other things,
that it is unconstitutional for a state to
determine that all minors under the
age of fifteen are too immature to make
an abortion decision without parental
approval.

1990　　In *Hodgson v. Minnesota* the US
Supreme Court holds that a two-parent
notice requirement is unconstitutional,
even with a judicial bypass procedure.

1992　　In *Planned Parenthood of Southeastern
Pennsylvania v. Casey* the US Supreme
Court holds that states may enact abor-
tion restrictions at any stage of preg-

nancy as long as such restrictions do not constitute an undue burden.

2007   In *Gonzales v. Carhart* the US Supreme Court holds that the Partial-Birth Abortion Ban Act of 2003, which restricts certain second- and third-trimester abortions, is constitutional.

> "The Court, in reaching its decision, was guided by the medical and legal history of abortion, as well as by a long line of constitutional privacy cases."

The Supreme Court Decriminalized Abortion in *Roe v. Wade*

J. Shoshanna Ehrlich

In the following viewpoint, a women's studies professor argues that the US Supreme Court's 1973 decision in Roe v. Wade, decriminalizing abortion, was the result of a long history of legal and medical grappling with the issue. The author contends that abortion in the first half of pregnancy was historically not a crime, but in the nineteenth century it became available only with medical permission. She claims that the women's movement pushed for the abortion decision to be recognized as a woman's right. J. Shoshanna Ehrlich is associate professor and department chair of women's studies at the University of Massachusetts Boston.

In 1973, in the landmark case of *Roe v. Wade*, the U.S. Supreme Court invalidated Texas's criminal abortion law, which barred a woman from terminating a pregnancy unless a doctor deter-

J. Shoshanna Ehrlich, "*Roe v. Wade*, 410 US 113 (1973)," *Encyclopedia of the Supreme Court of the United States*, 1st ed. Copyright © 2009 Cengage Learning.

mined it was necessary to save her life. Reasoning within a historical framework, the Court concluded that until fetal viability, the constitutional right of privacy protects a woman's ability to decide for herself whether or not to carry a pregnancy to term. Although some commentators assailed the decision for radically breaking from the past, the Court, in reaching its decision, was guided by the medical and legal history of abortion, as well as by a long line of constitutional privacy cases.

The Common-Law Quickening Rule

Recognizing "the sensitive and emotional nature of the abortion controversy," Justice Harry Blackmun, writing for the majority, anchored the decision in a historical framework that yielded insights into "man's attitudes toward the abortion procedure over the centuries." Perhaps seeking to deflect anticipated criticism that the decision abruptly broke with a fixed and continuous past, Blackmun began by noting that many may not appreciate the fact that the "restrictive criminal abortion laws in effect in a majority of States today are of relatively recent vintage."

As the discussed history reveals, under common law, an abortion performed prior to *quickening*—the moment when a woman first feels fetal movement—was not a crime. After quickening, which usually occurs in the fourth or fifth month of pregnancy, abortion could be punished as a crime; however, under the common law, abortion was not the equivalent of murder, and was punishable as a misdemeanor, rather than as a more serious felony offense. The quickening standard reflected both the biological fact that until a woman actually felt fetal movement, she could not know for certain whether or not she was pregnant, and the philosophical view that until it moved, the fetus was an inseparable part of the pregnant woman. . . .

During the second half of the nineteenth century, the common-law quickening rule came under attack, and states began enacting criminal abortion statues that, like the challenged Texas law, prohibited all abortions unless medically necessary

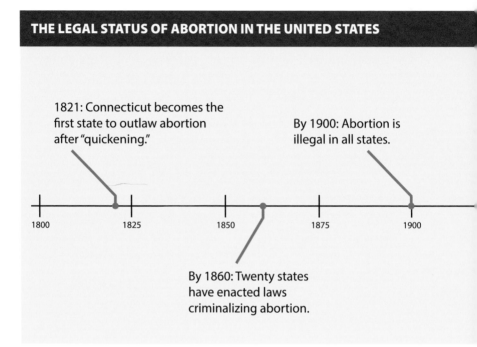

THE LEGAL STATUS OF ABORTION IN THE UNITED STATES

1821: Connecticut becomes the first state to outlaw abortion after "quickening."

By 1900: Abortion is illegal in all states.

1800   1825   1850   1875   1900

By 1860: Twenty states have enacted laws criminalizing abortion.

to save the life of a pregnant woman. It may come as a surprise to contemporary readers to learn that physicians were the driving force behind this nineteenth-century move to criminalize abortion in the United States. More specifically, it was the elite or "regular" physicians—those who had been formally trained in medical science—who spearheaded the reform campaign. . . .

The Implementation of Abortion Committees

Due mainly to the vigor of the doctors' campaign, by the start of the twentieth century, all states had made abortion a statutory crime unless medically necessary to save the life of a pregnant woman. Most statutes did not define the term *necessary*, and there was considerable disagreement among doctors about the scope of this therapeutic exception. Some read it very narrowly and would only perform an abortion when it was clear that con-

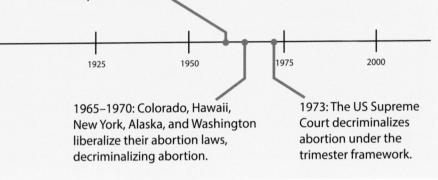

1960–1965: Arkansas, California, Colorado, Delaware, Georgia, Kansas, Maryland, New Mexico, North Carolina, Oregon, South Carolina, and Virginia modified their laws and allowed abortions to be performed by licensed physicians to protect the woman's physical and mental health, in the case of fetal defect, or when the pregnancy resulted from rape or incest.

1925   1950   1975   2000

1965–1970: Colorado, Hawaii, New York, Alaska, and Washington liberalize their abortion laws, decriminalizing abortion.

1973: The US Supreme Court decriminalizes abortion under the trimester framework.

tinuing the pregnancy would result in the death of the pregnant woman. Others read the exception more liberally to encompass what might be considered quality of life, rather than strictly life or death, considerations. This discretion generally worked to the disadvantage of poor women and women of color, who often lacked an ongoing relationship with a private doctor who might be willing to bend the rules for a trusted patient he had treated over many years.

Starting in the 1940s, in order to resolve the growing disagreements among doctors as to the permissible indications for performing a legal abortion, hospitals began establishing therapeutic abortion committees. To schedule an abortion for a patient, a doctor had to submit the case to the hospital's abortion committee for a determination as to whether it was "necessary" within the meaning of the law. According to [University of Illinois College of Law associate professor] Leslie J. Reagan, as increasing numbers of hospitals established therapeutic abortion committees, the concept of a legal abortion was equated with an abortion that had been formally approved by such a committee and performed in a hospital setting, as distinct from a doctor's office. In effect, these committees served to police the boundaries between legal and illegal procedures.

Despite their initial aim, these committees did not lead to the standardization of the practice of abortion, and in 1959, in an influential article entitled "Therapeutic Abortion: A Problem in Law and Medicine," authors Herbert L. Packer (1925–1972) and Ralph J. Gampell (1916–1988) concluded that "the abortion practice exhibits a dramatic variation between legal norm and social fact." Compounding this problem, committees also came under increasing pressure to limit the number of abortions they approved, and many imposed a quota system for the number of abortions they would approve in any given period. Once the limit had been reached, a woman's request for an abortion would most likely be denied, even if it fell within the narrow parameters of the law.

The Call for Liberalization

The gap between law and practice and the increasing strictness of therapeutic abortion committees led some doctors to call for the liberalization of the strict laws that their predecessors had fought so hard for a century earlier. Adding to their voices, in 1959 an elite group of lawyers under the auspices of the American Law Institute (ALI) also called for change. Toward this end, the ALI included a draft abortion provision in its Model Penal Code that essentially codified the liberal interpretation of the therapeutic abortion exception, thus allowing abortion in cases of rape and incest, when necessary to safeguard the physical or mental health (as well as the life) of the pregnant woman, and in cases of fetal anomalies.

By the time *Roe* was decided, about a quarter of the states had revised their criminal abortion statutes along the lines suggested by the ALI Model Penal Code. Although this was an important development, these liberalized laws simply expanded, or, perhaps more accurately, clarified the circumstances under which a doctor could lawfully perform an abortion. In short, they solidified the authority of doctors without transferring decision-making control to women.

Unwilling to settle for reforms that simply enlarged the scope of professional decision-making authority, women's rights activists called for a radical reconfiguration of the abortion right. Reflecting the growing influence of the women's movement, they reframed abortion as a right that women have in their own bodies. Linking reproductive control to women's social and legal equality, activists and a new generation of women lawyers and scholars sought the outright repeal of criminal abortion laws, thus launching a series of constitutional challenges that ultimately resulted in the landmark *Roe v. Wade* decision.

The Decriminalization of Abortion

In 1970, Jane Roe (a pseudonym) challenged the constitutionality of Texas's criminal abortion statute. Enacted in 1854, the Texas law, like others of its generation, banned all abortions unless medically necessary to save the life of the pregnant woman. Unable to avail herself of this exception, Roe argued that the law interfered with her constitutional right of personal privacy. Defending the law, the State of Texas asserted its right to protect the health of pregnant women and the life of the fetus by prohibiting abortion, except in narrow lifesaving circumstances.

In evaluating these competing claims, the Court agreed with the plaintiff that the Texas law abridged her right of personal privacy. Relying on a long line of cases reaching back to 1891 in which it had identified a right of privacy in a variety of contexts, including activities related to marriage, procreation, contraception, child rearing, and education, the Court held that the "right of privacy . . . founded in the Fourteenth Amendment's concept of personal liberty and restrictions upon state action . . . is broad enough to encompass a woman's decision whether or not to terminate a pregnancy." In so holding, the Court recognized "the detriment that the State would impose upon the pregnant woman by denying this choice," including psychological harm, the distress of bringing a child who is unwanted into the world, and the possible stigma of unwed motherhood.

This, however, was not the end of the Court's analysis. Although making clear that abortion is a fundamental right, the Court rejected the plaintiff's argument that the right is absolute, and instead held that a woman's right must be balanced against the interests of the state. In considering the asserted interests of the State of Texas, the Court disagreed with its claim that the fetus is a person within the meaning of the Constitution, and thus deserving of full legal protection. In rejecting the idea of fetal personhood, the Court reviewed the term *person* as it appears in the Constitution, and determined that it does not have "any possible pre-natal application." The Court also pointed out that if the fetus were a legal person, the therapeutic abortion exception would, in effect, be authorizing the saving of one life through the intentional destruction of another—an act the law would not sanction. The Court also declined to fix the start of life at the moment of conception, as it was urged to do by the State of Texas, stating that: "We need not resolve the difficult question of when life begins. When those trained in the respective disciplines of medicine, philosophy, and theology are unable to arrive at any consensus, the judiciary, at this point in the development of man's knowledge, is not in a position to speculate as to the answer."

The Balancing of Interests

Although declining to vest the fetus with a formal legal status, or declare when life begins, the Court did find that states do have a valid interest in protecting both the health of pregnant women and the potentiality of life, and that these interests can be taken into account in shaping the contours of the abortion right. Recognizing both the fundamental nature of the abortion

Norma McCorvey (left), also known as Jane Roe in the landmark 1973 Roe v. Wade *case, celebrates with lawyer Gloria Allred after sitting in on an abortion-related trial at the US Supreme Court.* © AP Images/J. Scott Applewhite.

right and the fact that pregnancy is a dynamic process, the Court held that these interests are not of sufficient magnitude throughout pregnancy to support state regulation of abortion. Rather, these interests grow in significance over the course of pregnancy, and become "compelling" at distinct stages of pregnancy, so as to support some limitations on the abortion right.

To accommodate the tension between a woman's constitutional right of choice and the interests of the state, the Court constructed its now famous trimester approach to the regulation of abortion, as follows: in the first trimester, the interests of the state are not of sufficient weight to justify intrusions on a woman's right of choice—it is without limitation; in the second trimester, when the procedure potentially increases in risk, the state's interest in the health of the pregnant woman becomes compelling and justifies regulations that are intended to protect her well-being;

finally, as a pregnancy enters the third trimester, and the fetus become viable, defined by the Court as being capable of "meaningful life outside the mother's womb," the state's interest in the potentiality of life becomes compelling, and it may prohibit abortion. However, the Court also made clear that the welfare of the pregnant woman always takes precedence over potential life, and a state must therefore permit third-trimester abortions that are necessary to protect the life or health of the woman.

In dissent, Justices Byron White and William Rehnquist took the Court to task for fashioning what they deemed to be a new substantive right. Grounded in a states' rights perspective, the dissenting justices essentially characterized the majority opinion as a usurpation of judicial authority through which the Court privileged the convenience of pregnant women over the right of states to express their respect for fetal life through the legislative process.

The Reaction to *Roe*

Abortion rights supporters were generally elated by the *Roe* decision. Although stopping short of declaring that women had an absolute right to make the abortion decision free from any state interference, the decision effectively repealed existing criminal bans. Accordingly, rather than simply expanding the circumstances under which abortions could lawfully be performed, decisional authority, at least until viability, had been shifted to the pregnant woman. As hoped for, women were now at the center of the abortion decision.

Reflecting the belief that reproduction is a matter of choice, rather than a biological imperative, and the closely related idea that women must be free to make choices about their lives without the constraints of gender stereotypes, abortion rights proponents began referring to themselves as *pro-choice* rather than *pro-abortion*. However, supporters also recognized that the decision was not self-actualizing, and that without working to ensure reliable access to safe and affordable abortions, *Roe*'s promise of reproductive choice would be an empty one for many women.

In contrast, abortion opponents were generally outraged by the *Roe* decision. Believing that the Court had "suddenly and irrationally decided to undermine something basic in American life," [according to sociologist Kristen Luker], they quickly implemented a two-pronged legal opposition strategy. They pursued an amendment to the U.S. Constitution that would either declare abortion a matter over which the states had authority or alternatively would vest the fetus with legal personhood, while also seeking to enact state laws to restrict a woman's right of choice. Taking the long view, they hoped that if these laws were eventually challenged in court, the abortion battle would be replayed before a differently constituted Supreme Court, which would either overturn *Roe* or significantly narrow the scope of the decision.

This legislative strategy resulted in a flurry of activity, and within a year of *Roe*, states across the country had enacted a wide variety of restrictive laws, including spousal- and parental-consent requirements, informed-consent requirements that were intended to encourage women to change their minds about abortion, and the elimination of public funding for abortion. These laws were promptly challenged on the ground that they interfered with a woman's fundamental right of privacy to decide for herself whether or not to carry a pregnancy to term. Relying upon the *Roe* trimester framework, the Court struck down most of these restrictive laws until 1992, when in *Planned Parenthood of Southeastern Pennsylvania v. Casey*, it repudiated the trimester standard in favor of the less-restrictive "undue burden" standard, thus giving states more freedom to regulate abortion. However, in the years leading up to *Casey*, and perhaps presaging this erosion of *Roe*, the Court, in a significant departure from its existing abortion jurisprudence, accepted the validity of laws restricting the rights of both young women and low-income women, by way of, respectively, parental-involvement requirements (subject to a judicial waiver option) and public-funding restrictions.

| "*Abortion has been the subject of much ethical thought from both pro-life and pro-choice perspectives.*"

Public Opinion on Abortion Is Influenced by Science and Ethics

Bonnie Steinbock

In the following viewpoint, a philosophy professor contends that public opinion on abortion falls into three camps: conservative, liberal, and moderate. She claims the difference in opinion on abortion among the three views has to do with differing scientific and ethical beliefs. She also considers the beliefs underpinning the current legal perspective on abortion. Bonnie Steinbock is a professor of philosophy at the University at Albany, State University of New York, and a founding faculty member of the Union-Mount Sinai Bioethics Program. She is the author of Life Before Birth: The Moral and Legal Status of Embryos and Fetuses.

Despite the legalization of abortion in 1973, the topic continues to be controversial and divisive in American politics.

Bonnie Steinbock, "Abortion," *From Birth to Death and Bench to Clinic: The Hastings Center Bioethics Briefing Book for Journalists, Policymakers, and Campaigns,* ed. Mary Crowley. The Hastings Center, 2008, pp. 1–4. Copyright © 2008 by The Hastings Center. All rights reserved. Reproduced by permission.

While the right to have an abortion has remained settled since then, the issue was again before the Supreme Court in 2007. The Court upheld a 2003 law banning a form of abortion called intact dilation and extraction, or "partial-birth abortion." At one end of the debate over this practice are those who regard abortion as murder—a despicable and heinous crime. At the other end are those who regard any attempt to restrict abortion as a violation of women's rights to privacy and bodily self-determination. Most Americans are somewhere in the middle.

Abortion has been the subject of much ethical thought from both pro-life and pro-choice perspectives. The central philosophical question concerns the moral status of the embryo and fetus. If the fetus is a person, with the same right to life as any human being who has been born, it would seem that very few, if any, abortions could be justified, because [it] is not morally permissible to kill children because they are unwanted or illegitimate or disabled. However, the morality of abortion is not necessarily settled so straightforwardly. Even if one accepts the argument that the fetus is a person, it does not automatically follow that it has a right to the use of the pregnant woman's body. Without that right, as [US philosopher] Judith Thomson has argued, abortion could be justified.

Public opinion on abortion falls into three camps— conservative, liberal, and moderate (or gradualist)—each of which draws on both science and ethical thinking.

The Conservative Opinion on Abortion

Conservatives regard the fetus as a human being, with the same rights as any human being who has been born, from implantation (when a pregnancy begins) onward. Some conservative groups— such as the Catholic Church—consider the fetus to be a human being with full moral rights even earlier, from conception onward.

Conception is regarded as the significant point because that is when the embryo develops its own unique genetic code, distinct

Pro-choice and pro-life activists demonstrate in front of the Missouri state capitol building. Since the legalization of abortion in 1973, the issue has remained highly divisive and controversial in US politics. © Joseph Sohm/Visions of America/Corbis.

from that of its mother or father, and thus from the egg or sperm. (This belief leads the Catholic Church to oppose some forms of contraception, such as the IUD [intrauterine device] and the "morning-after" pill, since they cause the death of the embryo by preventing implantation, even before clinical pregnancy has occurred.) The fetus changes dramatically during gestation but, on the conservative view, no stage is ever reached at which we can say, now we have a human being, whereas a day or a week or a month earlier we did not. Any attempt to place the onset of humanity at a particular moment—whether it be when brain waves appear, or the human form becomes distinct, or at quickening, sentience, or viability—is bound to be arbitrary because all of these stages will occur if the fetus is allowed to grow and develop.

A more recent antiabortion argument by [US philosopher] Don Marquis in 1989 differs from the traditional conservative view in that it is not based on the fetus's being human, nor even based on species membership. Rather, Marquis argues that abortion is wrong for the same reason that killing anyone is wrong—namely, that killing deprives its victim of a valuable future, what he calls "a future like ours." This raises two questions about what it is to have a future like ours. First, what precisely is involved in this notion? Does it essentially belong to rational, future-oriented, plan-making beings? If so, then killing most nonhuman animals would not be wrong, but neither would killing those who are severely developmentally disabled. Second, at what point does the life of a being with a future like ours start? If the important notion is the loss of one's future, at what point is there an identifiable victim? Here the biology of gestation becomes important.

After conception but prior to implantation, the embryo can still split into two (or more) distinct individuals. This makes it impossible to connect the loss of a future to any particular "victim" prior to implantation. This may seem irrelevant since prior to implantation, there is no clinical pregnancy, and, therefore, no possibility of abortion. However, its relevance becomes apparent when one realizes that some forms of contraception (like the IUD and the "morning-after" pill) cause the death of the embryo by preventing implantation. On the "future like ours" account, emergency contraception is permissible, which contrasts with the view of the Catholic Church.

The Liberal and Moderate Opinions on Abortion

Most liberals acknowledge that the fetus is human in a biological sense, but deny that this endows the fetus with full moral status or a right to life. In 1971, Judith Thomson gave a completely different pro-choice argument, claiming that even if the personhood of the fetus were granted, this would not settle the morality of abortion because the fetus's right to life does not necessarily give it a right to use the pregnant woman's body. No one, Thomson says, has the right to use your body unless you give him permission —not even if he needs it for life itself. At least in the case of rape, the pregnant woman has not given the fetus the right to use her body. (Thus, Thomson's argument, somewhat ironic for an article entitled "A Defense of Abortion," provides those who are generally anti-choice with a rationale for making an exception in the case of rape, as do many pro-lifers—though not the Catholic Church.) Thomson maintains that whether a woman ought to allow a fetus to remain in her body is a separate question from whether the fetus is a person with a right to life, and depends instead on the amount of sacrifice or burden it imposes on her.

More recently, in 2003, Margaret Little argued that while abortion is not murder, neither is it necessarily moral. A pregnant woman and her fetus are not strangers; she is biologically its mother. However, she may have conflicts of duties. For example, a woman's relationship to her children who have been born goes beyond mere biological connection and imposes stronger obligations. For this reason, their interests may trump those of the fetus. At the same time, even if the fetus is not a person, it is a "burgeoning human life," and as such is worthy of respect. Many women believe that bringing a child into the world when they are not able to nurture it would be disrespectful of human life. The main reason women choose abortion, according to Little, is that they think it would be wrong to have a child when they are not capable of being good mothers.

The moderate, or gradualist, agrees with the liberal that a one-celled zygote is not a human person, but agrees with the conservative that the late-gestation fetus is virtually identical to a born infant. Thus, the moderate thinks that early abortions are morally better than late ones and that the reasons for having one should be stronger as the pregnancy progresses. A reason that might justify an early abortion, such as not wanting to become a mother, would not justify an abortion in the seventh month to the moderate.

The Legal Perspective

In 1973 in *Roe v. Wade*, the United States Supreme Court based its finding of a woman's constitutional right to have an abortion

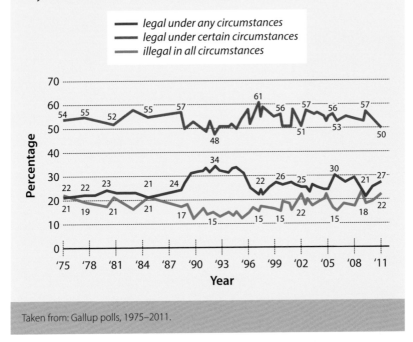

AMERICANS' VIEWS ON CIRCUMSTANCES UNDER WHICH ABORTION SHOULD BE LEGAL

Do you think abortions should be legal under any circumstances, legal only under certain circumstances, or illegal in all circumstances?

——— legal under any circumstances
——— legal under certain circumstances
——— illegal in all circumstances

Taken from: Gallup polls, 1975–2011.

up until viability on two factors: the legal status of the fetus and the woman's right to privacy. Concluding that outside of abortion law, the unborn had never been treated as full legal persons, the Court then looked to see if there were any state interests compelling enough to override a woman's right to make this personal decision for herself. It decided that there were none until the fetus became viable, somewhere between 24 and 28 weeks. At viability, the state's interest in protecting potential life trumps the woman's right to privacy, and at that point states may prohibit abortion altogether if they choose, unless continuing the pregnancy would threaten the woman's life or health.

FETAL DEVELOPMENT: A TIMELINE

The physiological development of the embryo and fetus during gestation does not alone determine the morality of abortion, but it is relevant to the argument over the moral status of the fetus. Gestation in humans has the duration of about 266 days.

0–22 hours	The first stage is **conception** or **fertilization**, a process that lasts about 22 hours and ends with syngamy, the merging of the parental chromosomes. Syngamy results in a single-celled zygote, which begins rapidly dividing. As many as 50% of conceptions end in early miscarriage.
6–13 days	The process of **implantation** begins on approximately the sixth day following fertilization and takes about a week. Once the embryo is implanted in the uterus, the pregnancy can be detected and is considered clinical. As implantation completes, the embryo develops a **primitive streak**, which is the precursor of the spinal cord and the nervous system. At the same time, the cells differentiate and become different kinds of tissue. This is known as **gastrulation**. Once implantation is completed, twinning—the division of the embryo into two or more genetically identical embryos—cannot occur.
12–16 weeks	Between 12 and 16 weeks, the fetus begins to look recognizably human. (Before then, it would be difficult to distinguish a human fetus from any other mammalian fetus.) Fetal movements, known as **quickening**, are felt by the mother early in the second trimester. By the end of the second trimester, the fetus may suck its thumb.
24–28 weeks	The fetus become **viable**, or capable of surviving outside the womb, in the third trimester, between 24 and 28 weeks. With a neonatal intensive care unit, a fetus of 28 weeks gestation age has about an 85% chance of survival. A 24-week-old fetus has only a 10% chance of survival. Even if a premature fetus survives, it is at risk for serious medical problems and lasting disability.

Taken from: Bonnie Steinbock, "Abortion," *From Birth to Death and Bench to Clinic: for Journalists, Policymakers, and Campaigns*, ed. Mary Crowley. Garrison, NY: The Hastings Center, 2008.

While the right to abortion has remained settled since *Roe v. Wade*, the right-to-life movement has recently focused on a particular abortion technique known to doctors as "intact dilation and extraction" and to the general public as "partial-birth abortion." In 2003, President [George W.] Bush signed into law a bill that banned the technique, describing it as a "gruesome, inhumane" procedure that is "never medically necessary to preserve a woman's health," in which a fetus is partially delivered alive and a physician performs "an overt act that the person knows will kill the partially delivered living fetus."

The law, which included no health exception, was found unconstitutional in 2005 but was upheld by the U.S. Supreme Court in the case of *Gonzales v. Carhart* in 2007. In her dissent, Justice Ruth Bader Ginsburg described the ruling as "alarming," and said that it "tolerates, indeed applauds, federal intervention to ban nationwide a procedure found necessary and proper in certain cases by the American College of Obstetricians and Gynecologists." For example, intact dilation and extraction is safer for the woman—and more likely to preserve her future fertility—than dilation and extraction is because dismembering the fetus in utero might puncture the uterus.

One of the more curious aspects of the law is that it makes no mention of the stage of gestation, prohibiting only intact dilation and extraction. It does not prohibit another method, dilation and extraction, which involves dismembering the fetus in the uterus, and can also be used beyond the first trimester. If the issue is how gruesome or inhumane the abortion is, drawing an ethical distinction between intact dilation and extraction and dilation and extraction in utero is puzzling. Moreover, many believe that the question of whether a particular procedure is medically indicated belongs to the woman's doctors, and not to the Congress of the United States. Opponents of the law argue that it could threaten some second-trimester abortions and that it is an attempt to intimidate doctors who perform abortions.

"The right of personal privacy includes the abortion decision, but . . . this right is not unqualified, and must be considered against important state interests in regulation."

The Right to Privacy Protects a Woman's Right to Choose Abortion

The Supreme Court's Decision

Harry Blackmun

In the following viewpoint, a US Supreme Court justice argues that the right to privacy protects a woman's right to abortion. The author recounts the history of abortion laws in the United States, noting that the state laws at the time of Roe v. Wade *were more restrictive than they had been in the past. He considers and rejects three reasons offered for the existence of a Texas law criminalizing abortion. Rejecting the notion of the fetus as a person, he nonetheless notes that there is a compelling interest for the state to protect fetal life after the end of the second trimester and to protect the life of the mother after the end of the first trimester, thus allowing increasing restrictions in the second and third trimesters. Harry*

Harry Blackmun, Opinion of the Court, *Roe v. Wade*, US Supreme Court, January 22, 1973.

Blackmun served as an associate justice of the US Supreme Court from 1970 to 1994.

The principal thrust of appellant's attack on the Texas statutes is that they improperly invade a right, said to be possessed by the pregnant woman, to choose to terminate her pregnancy. Appellant would discover this right in the concept of personal "liberty" embodied in the Fourteenth Amendment's Due Process Clause; or in personal, marital, familial, and sexual privacy said to be protected by the Bill of Rights or its penumbras or among those rights reserved to the people by the Ninth Amendment. Before addressing this claim, we feel it desirable briefly to survey, in several aspects, the history of abortion, for such insight as that history may afford us, and then to examine the state purposes and interests behind the criminal abortion laws.

The Historical View on Abortion

It perhaps is not generally appreciated that the restrictive criminal abortion laws in effect in a majority of States today are of relatively recent vintage. Those laws, generally proscribing abortion or its attempt at any time during pregnancy except when necessary to preserve the pregnant woman's life, are not of ancient or even of common law origin. Instead, they derive from statutory changes effected, for the most part, in the latter half of the 19th century. . . .

At the time of the adoption of our Constitution, and throughout the major portion of the 19th century, abortion was viewed with less disfavor than under most American statutes currently in effect. Phrasing it another way, a woman enjoyed a substantially broader right to terminate a pregnancy than she does in most States today. At least with respect to the early stage of pregnancy, and very possibly without such a limitation, the opportunity to make this choice was present in this country well into the 19th century. Even later, the law continued for some time to treat less punitively an abortion procured in early pregnancy. . . .

The Three Reasons for Criminal Abortion Laws

Three reasons have been advanced to explain historically the enactment of criminal abortion laws in the 19th century and to justify their continued existence.

It has been argued occasionally that these laws were the product of a Victorian social concern to discourage illicit sexual conduct. Texas, however, does not advance this justification in the present case, and it appears that no court or commentator has taken the argument seriously....

A second reason is concerned with abortion as a medical procedure. When most criminal abortion laws were first enacted, the procedure was a hazardous one for the woman. This was particularly true prior to the development of antisepsis. Antiseptic techniques, of course, were based on discoveries by [British surgeon Joseph] Lister, [French chemist Louis] Pasteur, and others first announced in 1867, but were not generally accepted and employed until about the turn of the century. Abortion mortality was high. Even after 1900, and perhaps until as late as the development of antibiotics in the 1940's, standard modern techniques such as dilation and curettage were not nearly so safe as they are today. Thus, it has been argued that a State's real concern in enacting a criminal abortion law was to protect the pregnant woman, that is, to restrain her from submitting to a procedure that placed her life in serious jeopardy.

Modern medical techniques have altered this situation. Appellants and various *amici* [parties giving unsolicited testimony to the court] refer to medical data indicating that abortion in early pregnancy, that is, prior to the end of the first trimester, although not without its risk, is now relatively safe. Mortality rates for women undergoing early abortions, where the procedure is legal, appear to be as low as or lower than the rates for normal childbirth. Consequently, any interest of the State in protecting the woman from an inherently hazardous procedure, except when it would be equally dangerous for her to forgo it,

Many pro-life activists argue that a person's life begins at conception, and thusly should be granted "personhood" and protected equally under the US Constitution. © Alex Wong/Getty Images.

has largely disappeared. Of course, important state interests in the areas of health and medical standards do remain. The State has a legitimate interest in seeing to it that abortion, like any other medical procedure, is performed under circumstances that insure maximum safety for the patient. This interest obviously extends at least to the performing physician and his staff, to the facilities involved, to the availability of after-care, and to adequate provision for any complication or emergency that might arise. The prevalence of high mortality rates at illegal "abortion mills" strengthens, rather than weakens, the State's interest in regulating the conditions under which abortions are performed. Moreover, the risk to the woman increases as her pregnancy continues. Thus, the State retains a definite interest in protecting the woman's own health and safety when an abortion is proposed at a late stage of pregnancy.

The third reason is the State's interest—some phrase it in terms of duty—in protecting prenatal life. Some of the argument for this justification rests on the theory that a new human life is present from the moment of conception. The State's interest and general obligation to protect life then extends, it is argued, to prenatal life. Only when the life of the pregnant mother herself is at stake, balanced against the life she carries within her, should the interest of the embryo or fetus not prevail. Logically, of course, a legitimate state interest in this area need not stand or fall on acceptance of the belief that life begins at conception or at some other point prior to live birth. In assessing the State's interest, recognition may be given to the less rigid claim that as long as at least potential life is involved, the State may assert interests beyond the protection of the pregnant woman alone. . . .

The Right to Privacy

The Constitution does not explicitly mention any right of privacy. In a line of decisions, however, going back perhaps as far as *Union Pacific R. Co. v. Botsford* (1891), the Court has recognized that a right of personal privacy, or a guarantee of certain areas or zones of privacy, does exist under the Constitution. In varying contexts, the Court or individual Justices have, indeed, found at least the roots of that right in the First Amendment, in the Fourth and Fifth Amendments, in the penumbras of the Bill of Rights, in the Ninth Amendment, or in the concept of liberty guaranteed by the first section of the Fourteenth Amendment. These decisions make it clear that only personal rights that can be deemed "fundamental" or "implicit in the concept of ordered liberty," *Palko v. Connecticut*, (1937), are included in this guarantee of personal privacy. They also make it clear that the right has some extension to activities relating to marriage, procreation, contraception, family relationships, and childrearing and education.

This right of privacy, whether it be founded in the Fourteenth Amendment's concept of personal liberty and restrictions upon state action, as we feel it is, or, as the District Court determined, in the Ninth Amendment's reservation of rights to the people, is broad enough to encompass a woman's decision whether or not to terminate her pregnancy. The detriment that the State would impose upon the pregnant woman by denying this choice altogether is apparent. Specific and direct harm medically diagnosable even in early pregnancy may be involved. Maternity, or additional offspring, may force upon the woman a distressful life and future. Psychological harm may be imminent. Mental and physical health may be taxed by child care. There is also the distress, for all concerned, associated with the unwanted child, and there is the problem of bringing a child into a family already unable, psychologically and otherwise, to care for it. In other cases, as in this one, the additional difficulties and continuing stigma of unwed motherhood may be involved. All these are factors the woman and her responsible physician necessarily will consider in consultation.

On the basis of elements such as these, appellant and some *amici* argue that the woman's right is absolute and that she is entitled to terminate her pregnancy at whatever time, in whatever way, and for whatever reason she alone chooses. With this we do not agree. Appellant's arguments that Texas either has no valid interest at all in regulating the abortion decision, or no interest strong enough to support any limitation upon the woman's sole determination, are unpersuasive. The Court's decisions recognizing a right of privacy also acknowledge that some state regulation in areas protected by that right is appropriate. As noted above, a State may properly assert important interests in safeguarding health, in maintaining medical standards, and in protecting potential life. At some point in pregnancy, these respective interests become sufficiently compelling to sustain regulation of the factors that govern the abortion decision. The privacy right involved, therefore, cannot be said to be absolute. In fact, it is not clear to us that the claim asserted by some *amici* that one has an unlimited right to do with one's body as one pleases bears a close relationship to the right of privacy previously articulated in the Court's decisions. The Court has refused to recognize an unlimited right of this kind in the past.

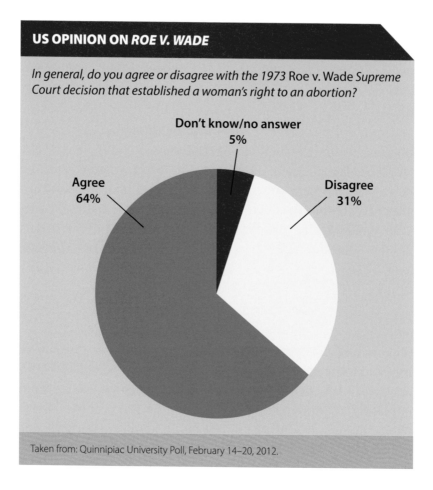

US OPINION ON *ROE V. WADE*

In general, do you agree or disagree with the 1973 Roe v. Wade *Supreme Court decision that established a woman's right to an abortion?*

Don't know/no answer
5%

Agree
64%

Disagree
31%

Taken from: Quinnipiac University Poll, February 14–20, 2012.

We, therefore, conclude that the right of personal privacy includes the abortion decision, but that this right is not unqualified, and must be considered against important state interests in regulation. . . .

The Issue of Personhood

The appellee and certain *amici* argue that the fetus is a "person" within the language and meaning of the Fourteenth Amendment. In support of this, they outline at length and in detail the well known facts of fetal development. If this suggestion of personhood is established, the appellant's case, of course, collapses, for the fetus' right to life would then be guaranteed specifically by the Amendment. The appellant conceded as much on reargument. On the other hand, the appellee conceded on reargument that no case could be cited that holds that a fetus is a person within the meaning of the Fourteenth Amendment.

The Constitution does not define "person" in so many words. Section 1 of the Fourteenth Amendment contains three references to "person." The first, in defining "citizens," speaks of "persons born or naturalized in the United States." The word also appears both in the Due Process Clause and in the Equal Protection Clause. "Person" is used in other places in the Constitution. . . . But in nearly all these instances, the use of the word is such that it has application only post-natally. None indicates, with any assurance, that it has any possible pre-natal application.

All this, together with our observation that, throughout the major portion of the 19th century, prevailing legal abortion practices were far freer than they are today, persuades us that the word "person," as used in the Fourteenth Amendment, does not include the unborn. . . .

Texas urges that, apart from the Fourteenth Amendment, life begins at conception and is present throughout pregnancy, and that, therefore, the State has a compelling interest in protecting that life from and after conception. We need not resolve the difficult question of when life begins. When those trained in the respective disciplines of medicine, philosophy, and theology are unable to arrive at any consensus, the judiciary, at this point in the development of man's knowledge, is not in a position to speculate as to the answer. . . .

The State's Interests

In view of all this, we do not agree that, by adopting one theory of life, Texas may override the rights of the pregnant woman that are at stake. We repeat, however, that the State does have an important and legitimate interest in preserving and protecting the health of the pregnant woman, whether she be a resident of the State or a nonresident who seeks medical consultation and treatment there, and that it has still *another* important and legitimate interest in protecting the potentiality of human life. These interests are separate and distinct. Each grows in substantiality as the woman approaches term and, at a point during pregnancy, each becomes "compelling."

With respect to the State's important and legitimate interest in the health of the mother, the "compelling" point, in the light of present medical knowledge, is at approximately the end of the first trimester. This is so because of the now-established medical fact . . . that, until the end of the first trimester mortality in abortion may be less than mortality in normal childbirth. It follows that, from and after this point, a State may regulate the abortion procedure to the extent that the regulation reasonably relates to the preservation and protection of maternal health. Examples of permissible state regulation in this area are requirements as to the qualifications of the person who is to perform the abortion; as to the licensure of that person; as to the facility in which the procedure is to be performed, that is, whether it must be a hospital or may be a clinic or some other place of less-than-hospital status; as to the licensing of the facility; and the like.

This means, on the other hand, that, for the period of pregnancy prior to this "compelling" point, the attending physician, in consultation with his patient, is free to determine, without regulation by the State, that, in his medical judgment, the patient's pregnancy should be terminated. If that decision is reached, the judgment may be effectuated by an abortion free of interference by the State.

With respect to the State's important and legitimate interest in potential life, the "compelling" point is at viability. This is so because the fetus then presumably has the capability of meaningful life outside the mother's womb. State regulation protective of fetal life after viability thus has both logical and biological justifications. If the State is interested in protecting fetal life after viability, it may go so far as to proscribe abortion during that period, except when it is necessary to preserve the life or health of the mother. . . .

A state criminal abortion statute of the current Texas type, that excepts from criminality only a lifesaving procedure on behalf of the mother, without regard to pregnancy stage and without recognition of the other interests involved, is violative of the Due Process Clause of the Fourteenth Amendment.

(a) For the stage prior to approximately the end of the first trimester, the abortion decision and its effectuation must be left to the medical judgment of the pregnant woman's attending physician.

(b) For the stage subsequent to approximately the end of the first trimester, the State, in promoting its interest in the health of the mother, may, if it chooses, regulate the abortion procedure in ways that are reasonably related to maternal health.

(c) For the stage subsequent to viability, the State in promoting its interest in the potentiality of human life may, if it chooses, regulate, and even proscribe, abortion except where it is necessary, in appropriate medical judgment, for the preservation of the life or health of the mother.

> "The State does not have the constitutional authority to give a third party an absolute, and possibly arbitrary, veto over the decision of the physician and his patient."

Requiring Parental or Spousal Consent for Abortion Is Unconstitutional

The Supreme Court's Decision

Harry Blackmun

In the following viewpoint, a US Supreme Court justice contends that states may not enact restrictions on abortion that require women to get spousal or parental consent. The author contends that the right identified in Roe v. Wade *applies to minors as well as adults. Just as the state may not give a husband ultimate veto power over his wife's decision to have an abortion, neither can the state give parents ultimate veto power over a minor's decision to have an abortion without violating her right to privacy. Harry Blackmun was associate justice of the US Supreme Court from 1970 until his retirement in 1994.*

Harry Blackmun, Opinion of the Court, *Planned Parenthood of Central Missouri v. Danforth*, US Supreme Court, July 1, 1976.

This case is a logical and anticipated corollary to *Roe v. Wade* (1973), and *Doe v. Bolton* (1973), for it raises issues secondary to those that were then before the Court. Indeed, some of the questions now presented were forecast and reserved in *Roe* and *Doe*. . . .

The Issue of Regulation Under *Roe*

In June, 1974, somewhat more than a year after *Roe* and *Doe* had been decided, Missouri's 77th General Assembly, in its Second Regular Session, enacted House Committee Substitute for House Bill No. 1211 (hereinafter Act). The legislation was approved by the Governor on June 14, 1974, and became effective immediately. . . . It imposes a structure for the control and regulation of abortions in Missouri during all stages of pregnancy. . . .

In *Roe v. Wade*, the Court concluded that the

right of privacy, whether it be founded in the Fourteenth Amendment's concept of personal liberty and restrictions upon state action, as we feel it is, or, as the District Court determined, in the Ninth Amendment's reservation of rights to the people, is broad enough to encompass a woman's decision whether or not to terminate her pregnancy.

It emphatically rejected, however, the proffered argument

that the woman's right is absolute, and that she is entitled to terminate her pregnancy at whatever time, in whatever way, and for whatever reason, she alone chooses.

Instead, this right "must be considered against important state interests in regulation." . . .

The Requirement of Spousal Consent

In *Roe* and *Doe*, we specifically reserved decision on the question whether a requirement for consent by the father of the fetus, by the spouse, or by the parents, or a parent, of an unmarried minor, may be constitutionally imposed. We now hold that the

State may not constitutionally require the consent of the spouse, as is specified under § 3(3) of the Missouri Act, as a condition for abortion during the first 12 weeks of pregnancy. . . .

It seems manifest that, ideally, the decision to terminate a pregnancy should be one concurred in by both the wife and her husband. No marriage may be viewed as harmonious or successful if the marriage partners are fundamentally divided on so important and vital an issue. But it is difficult to believe that the goal of fostering mutuality and trust in a marriage, and of strengthening the marital relationship and the marriage institution, will be achieved by giving the husband a veto power exercisable for any reason whatsoever or for no reason at all. Even if the State had the ability to delegate to the husband a power it itself could not exercise, it is not at all likely that such action would further, as the District Court majority phrased it, the "interest of the state in protecting the mutuality of decisions vital to the marriage relationship."

We recognize, of course, that, when a woman, with the approval of her physician but without the approval of her husband, decides to terminate her pregnancy, it could be said that she is acting unilaterally. The obvious fact is that, when the wife and the husband disagree on this decision, the view of only one of the two marriage partners can prevail. Inasmuch as it is the woman who physically bears the child and who is the more directly and immediately affected by the pregnancy, as between the two, the balance weighs in her favor.

> We conclude that § 3(3) of the Missouri Act is inconsistent with the standards enunciated in *Roe v. Wade*, and is unconstitutional. . . .

The Requirement of Parental Consent

Section 3(4) requires, with respect to the first 12 weeks of pregnancy, where the woman is unmarried and under the age of 18 years, the written consent of a parent or person *in loco parentis*

Children's Rights and Parental Authority

The issue of greatest concern for many parents has been their children's sexual education and involvement. A particularly contentious area has been parents' desire to intervene in a daughter's decision to have an abortion. The confluence of minors obtaining abortions and parental rights and responsibilities for medical care has led to a patchwork quilt of laws concerning medical procedures and parental authority. For example, in most states it is illegal for minors to get their ears pierced without parental consent. However, in many states government officials take the position that children's rights to serious medical procedures outweigh parental authority.

Colby May, "Parental Rights,"
World & I, May 1997.

[in the place of a parent] unless, again, "the abortion is certified by a licensed physician as necessary in order to preserve the life of the mother." It is to be observed that only one parent need consent.

The appellees defend the statute in several ways. They point out that the law properly may subject minors to more stringent limitations than are permissible with respect to adults, and they cite, among other cases, *Prince v. Massachusetts* [1944] and *McKeiver v. Pennsylvania* (1971). Missouri law, it is said, "is replete with provisions reflecting the interest of the state in assuring the welfare of minors," citing statutes relating to a guardian *ad litem* [for the lawsuit] for a court proceeding, to the care of delinquent and neglected children, to child labor, and to compulsory education. Certain decisions are considered by the State to be outside the scope of a minor's ability to act in his own best interest or in the interest of the public, citing statutes proscribing

Planned Parenthood, the United States' largest provider of reproductive health services, has been at the forefront of women's rights legislation. © AP Images/Charles Krupa.

the sale of firearms and deadly weapons to minors without parental consent, and other statutes relating to minors' exposure to certain types of literature, the purchase by pawnbrokers of property from minors, and the sale of cigarettes and alcoholic beverages to minors. It is pointed out that the record contains testimony to the effect that children of tender years (even ages 10 and 11) have sought abortions. Thus, a State's permitting a child to obtain an abortion without the counsel of an adult

> who has responsibility or concern for the child would constitute an irresponsible abdication of the State's duty to protect the welfare of minors.

Parental discretion, too, has been protected from unwarranted or unreasonable interference from the State, citing *Meyer v. Nebraska* (1923); *Pierce v. Society of Sisters* (1925);

Wisconsin v. Yoder (1972). Finally, it is said that § 3(4) imposes no additional burden on the physician, because, even prior to the passage of the Act, the physician would require parental consent before performing an abortion on a minor.

The appellants, in their turn, emphasize that no other Missouri statute specifically requires the additional consent of a minor's parent for medical or surgical treatment, and that, in Missouri, a minor legally may consent to medical services for pregnancy (excluding abortion), venereal disease, and drug abuse. The result of § 3(4), it is said, "is the ultimate supremacy of the parents' desires over those of the minor child, the pregnant patient." It is noted that, in Missouri, a woman under the age of 18 who marries with parental consent does not require parental consent to abort, and yet her contemporary who has chosen not to marry must obtain parental approval. The District Court majority recognized that, in contrast to § 3(3), the State's interest in protecting the mutuality of a marriage relationship is not present with respect to § 3(4). It found "a compelling basis," however, in the State's interest "in safeguarding the authority of the family relationship." The dissenting judge observed that one could not seriously argue that a minor must submit to an abortion if her parents insist, and he could not see

> why she would not be entitled to the same right of self-determination now explicitly accorded to adult women, provided she is sufficiently mature to understand the procedure and to make an intelligent assessment of her circumstances with the advice of her physician. . . .

The Third-Party Veto Power

The State may not impose a blanket provision, such as § 3(4), requiring the consent of a parent or person *in loco parentis* as a condition for abortion of an unmarried minor during the first 12 weeks of her pregnancy. Just as with the requirement of consent from the spouse, so here, the State does not have the constitutional authority to give a third party an absolute, and possibly arbitrary, veto over the decision of the physician and his patient to terminate the patient's pregnancy, regardless of the reason for withholding the consent.

Constitutional rights do not mature and come into being magically only when one attains the state-defined age of majority. Minors, as well as adults, are protected by the Constitution, and possess constitutional rights. The Court indeed, however, long has recognized that the State has somewhat broader authority to regulate the activities of children than of adults. It remains, then, to examine whether there is any significant state interest in conditioning an abortion on the consent of a parent or person *in loco parentis* that is not present in the case of an adult.

One suggested interest is the safeguarding of the family unit and of parental authority. It is difficult, however, to conclude that providing a parent with absolute power to overrule a determination, made by the physician and his minor patient, to terminate the patient's pregnancy will serve to strengthen the family unit. Neither is it likely that such veto power will enhance parental authority or control where the minor and the nonconsenting parent are so fundamentally in conflict and the very existence of the pregnancy already has fractured the family structure. Any independent interest the parent may have in the termination of the minor daughter's pregnancy is no more weighty than the right of privacy of the competent minor mature enough to have become pregnant.

We emphasize that our holding that § 3(4) is invalid does not suggest that every minor, regardless of age or maturity, may give effective consent for termination of her pregnancy. The fault with § (4) is that it imposes a special consent provision, exercisable by a person other than the woman and her physician, as a prerequisite to a minor's termination of her pregnancy, and does so without a sufficient justification for the restriction. It violates the strictures of *Roe* and *Doe*.

"If the State decides to require a
pregnant minor to obtain one or both
parents' consent to an abortion, it also
must provide an alternative."

States May Require Parental Consent for Abortion If an Alternative Form of Authorization Is Also Available

The Supreme Court's Decision

Lewis F. Powell Jr.

In the following viewpoint, a US Supreme Court justice argues that states may require parental consent in order for a minor to get an abortion, as long as the state provides an alternative procedure for the minor to obtain permission. The author notes that the court's previous decisions support the unique treatment of minors under the law, including respect for the role of parents. He recognizes that the court determined in Planned Parenthood of Central Missouri v. Danforth *(1976) that the state may not require parental consent with no alternatives, but he concludes states may require parental*

Lewis F. Powell Jr., Opinion of the Court, *Bellotti v. Baird*, US Supreme Court, July 2, 1979.

consent as long as they allow the possibility for anonymous and quick judicial authorization as well. Lewis F. Powell Jr. was an associate justice on the US Supreme Court from 1972 until 1987.

A child, merely on account of his minority, is not beyond the protection of the Constitution. As the Court said in *In re Gault* (1967), "whatever may be their precise impact, neither the Fourteenth Amendment nor the Bill of Rights is for adults alone." This observation, of course, is but the beginning of the analysis. The Court long has recognized that the status of minors under the law is unique in many respects. As Mr. Justice [Felix] Frankfurter aptly put it: "Children have a very special place in life which law should reflect. Legal theories and their phrasing in other cases readily lead to fallacious reasoning if uncritically transferred to determination of a State's duty towards children" [*May v. Anderson* (1953) (concurring opinion)]. The unique role in our society of the family, the institution by which "we inculcate and pass down many of our most cherished values, moral and cultural" [*Moore v. East Cleveland* (1977) (plurality opinion)], requires that constitutional principles be applied with sensitivity and flexibility to the special needs of parents and children. We have recognized three reasons justifying the conclusion that the constitutional rights of children cannot be equated with those of adults: the peculiar vulnerability of children; their inability to make critical decisions in an informed, mature manner; and the importance of the parental role in child rearing.

The Constitutional Rights of Children

The Court's concern for the vulnerability of children is demonstrated in its decisions dealing with minors' claims to constitutional protection against deprivations of liberty or property interests by the State. With respect to many of these claims, we have concluded that the child's right is virtually coextensive with that of an adult. For example, the Court has held that the Fourteenth Amendment's guarantee against the deprivation of liberty without due process of law is applicable to children in juvenile delinquency proceedings. In particular, minors involved in such proceedings are entitled to adequate notice, the assistance of counsel, and the opportunity to confront their accusers. They can be found guilty only upon proof beyond a reasonable doubt, and they may assert the privilege against compulsory self-incrimination. Similarly, in *Goss v. Lopez* (1975), the Court held that children may not be deprived of certain property interests without due process.

These rulings have not been made on the uncritical assumption that the constitutional rights of children are indistinguishable from those of adults. Indeed, our acceptance of juvenile courts distinct from the adult criminal justice system assumes that juvenile offenders constitutionally may be treated differently from adults. In order to preserve this separate avenue for dealing with minors, the Court has said that hearings in juvenile delinquency cases need not necessarily "'conform with all of the requirements of a criminal trial or even of the usual administrative hearing'" [*In re Gault*, quoting *Kent v. United States* (1966)]. Thus, juveniles are not constitutionally entitled to trial by jury in delinquency adjudications. Viewed together, our cases show that although children generally are protected by the same constitutional guarantees against governmental deprivations as are adults, the State is entitled to adjust its legal system to account for children's vulnerability and their needs for "concern, . . . sympathy, and . . . paternal attention."

Limits on Children's Freedom

Second, the Court has held that the States validly may limit the freedom of children to choose for themselves in the making of important, affirmative choices with potentially serious consequences. These rulings have been grounded in the recognition that, during the formative years of childhood and adolescence, minors often lack the experience, perspective, and judgment to recognize and avoid choices that could be detrimental to them.

Ginsberg v. New York (1968), illustrates well the Court's concern over the inability of children to make mature choices, as the First Amendment rights involved are clear examples of constitutionally protected freedoms of choice. At issue was a criminal conviction for selling sexually oriented magazines to a minor under the age of 17 in violation of a New York state law. It was conceded that the conviction could not have stood under the First Amendment if based upon a sale of the same material to an adult. Notwithstanding the importance the Court always has attached to First Amendment rights, it concluded that "even where there is an invasion of protected freedoms 'the power of the state to control the conduct of children reaches beyond the scope of its authority over adults . . .'" [quoting *Prince v. Massachusetts* (1944)]. The Court was convinced that the New York Legislature rationally could conclude that the sale to children of the magazines in question presented a danger against which they should be guarded. It therefore rejected the argument that the New York law violated the constitutional rights of minors.

The Role of Parents

Third, the guiding role of parents in the upbringing of their children justifies limitations on the freedoms of minors. The State commonly protects its youth from adverse governmental action and from their own immaturity by requiring parental consent to or involvement in important decisions by minors. But an additional and more important justification for state deference to parental control over children is that "[t]he child is not the mere creature of the State; those who nurture him and direct his destiny have the right, coupled with the high duty, to recognize and prepare him for additional obligations" [*Pierce v. Society of Sisters* (1925)]. "The duty to prepare the child for 'additional obligations' . . . must be read to include the inculcation of moral standards, religious beliefs, and elements of good citizenship" [*Wisconsin v. Yoder* (1972)]. This affirmative process of teach-

The US Supreme Court ruled that if a state is to require a minor to seek parental consent before having an abortion, the state must also provide an alternate means of consent. © Kikor/Blend Images/Getty Images.

ing, guiding, and inspiring by precept and example is essential to the growth of young people into mature, socially responsible citizens.

We have believed in this country that this process, in large part, is beyond the competence of impersonal political institutions. Indeed, affirmative sponsorship of particular ethical, religious, or political beliefs is something we expect the State not to attempt in a society constitutionally committed to the ideal of individual liberty and freedom of choice. Thus, "[i]t is cardinal with us that the custody, care and nurture of the child reside first in the parents, whose primary function and freedom include preparation for obligations the state can neither supply nor hinder" [*Prince v. Massachusetts*].

Unquestionably, there are many competing theories about the most effective way for parents to fulfill their central role in assisting their children on the way to responsible adulthood. While we do not pretend any special wisdom on this subject, we cannot ignore that central to many of these theories, and deeply rooted in our Nation's history and tradition, is the belief that the parental role implies a substantial measure of authority over one's children. Indeed, "constitutional interpretation has consistently recognized that the parents' claim to authority in their own household to direct the rearing of their children is basic in the structure of our society" [*Ginsberg v. New York*].

Properly understood, then, the tradition of parental authority is not inconsistent with our tradition of individual liberty; rather, the former is one of the basic presuppositions of the latter. Legal restrictions on minors, especially those supportive of the parental role, may be important to the child's chances for the full growth and maturity that make eventual participation in a free society meaningful and rewarding. Under the Constitution, the State can "properly conclude that parents and others, teachers for example, who have [the] primary responsibility for children's well-being are entitled to the support of laws designed to aid discharge of that responsibility" [*Ginsberg v. New York*]. . . .

As immature minors often lack the ability to make fully informed choices that take account of both immediate and long-range consequences, a State reasonably may determine that parental consultation often is desirable and in the best interest of the minor. It may further determine, as a general proposition, that such consultation is particularly desirable with respect to the abortion decision—one that for some people raises profound moral and religious concerns. As MR. JUSTICE [Potter] STEWART wrote in concurrence in *Planned Parenthood of Central Missouri v. Danforth* [1976]:

> There can be little doubt that the State furthers a constitutionally permissible end by encouraging an unmarried pregnant minor to seek the help and advice of her parents in making the

very important decision whether or not to bear a child. That is a grave decision, and a girl of tender years, under emotional stress, may be ill-equipped to make it without mature advice and emotional support. It seems unlikely that she will obtain adequate counsel and support from the attending physician at an abortion clinic, where abortions for pregnant minors frequently take place.

States Must Provide Minors with an Alternative Authorization for Abortion

But we are concerned here with a constitutional right to seek an abortion. The abortion decision differs in important ways from other decisions that may be made during minority. The need to preserve the constitutional right and the unique nature of the abortion decision, especially when made by a minor, require a State to act with particular sensitivity when it legislates to foster parental involvement in this matter.

The pregnant minor's options are much different from those facing a minor in other situations, such as deciding whether to marry. A minor not permitted to marry before the age of majority is required simply to postpone her decision. She and her intended spouse may preserve the opportunity for later marriage should they continue to desire it. A pregnant adolescent, however, cannot preserve for long the possibility of aborting, which effectively expires in a matter of weeks from the onset of pregnancy.

Moreover, the potentially severe detriment facing a pregnant woman is not mitigated by her minority. Indeed, considering her probable education, employment skills, financial resources, and emotional maturity, unwanted motherhood may be exceptionally burdensome for a minor. In addition, the fact of having a child brings with it adult legal responsibility, for parenthood, like attainment of the age of majority, is one of the traditional criteria for the termination of the legal disabilities of minority. In sum,

SUPPORT FOR PARENTAL CONSENT LAWS FOR MINORS IN THE UNITED STATES, 2009		
Among those who believe abortion should be . . .	**Favor**	**Oppose**
Legal	71%	27%
Illegal	83%	13%

Taken from: Pew Research Center, Annual Religion and Public Life Survey, 2009.

there are few situations in which denying a minor the right to make an important decision will have consequences so grave and indelible.

Yet, an abortion may not be the best choice for the minor. The circumstances in which this issue arises will vary widely. In a given case, alternatives to abortion, such as marriage to the father of the child, arranging for its adoption, or assuming the responsibilities of motherhood with the assured support of family, may be feasible and relevant to the minor's best interests. Nonetheless, the abortion decision is one that simply cannot be postponed, or it will be made by default with far-reaching consequences.

For these reasons, as we held in *Planned Parenthood of Central Missouri v. Danforth,* "the State may not impose a blanket provision . . . requiring the consent of a parent or person *in loco parentis* as a condition for abortion of an unmarried minor during the first 12 weeks of her pregnancy." Although . . . such deference to parents may be permissible with respect to other choices facing a minor, the unique nature and consequences of the abortion decision make it inappropriate "to give a third party an absolute, and possibly arbitrary, veto over the decision of the physician and his patient to terminate the patient's pregnancy, regardless of the reason for withholding the consent." We therefore conclude that if the State decides to require a pregnant minor to obtain one or both parents' consent to an abortion, it also must provide an alternative procedure whereby authorization for the abortion can be obtained.

A pregnant minor is entitled in such a proceeding to show either: (1) that she is mature enough and well enough informed to make her abortion decision, in consultation with her physician, independently of her parents' wishes; or (2) that even if she is not able to make this decision independently, the desired abortion would be in her best interests. The proceeding in which this showing is made must assure that a resolution of the issue, and any appeals that may follow, will be completed with anonymity and sufficient expedition to provide an effective opportunity for an abortion to be obtained. In sum, the procedure must ensure that the provision requiring parental consent does not in fact amount to the "absolute, and possibly arbitrary, veto" that was found impermissible in *Danforth*.

*"A statute which . . . [places] a
substantial obstacle in the path of a
woman's choice cannot be considered
a permissible means of serving its
legitimate ends."*

States May Enact Abortion Restrictions That Do Not Pose Substantial Obstacles

The Supreme Court's Decision

Sandra Day O'Connor

*In the following viewpoint, a US Supreme Court justice argues that
the central holding of* Roe v. Wade *supporting a woman's right to
choose abortion prior to fetus viability is valid. However, the author rejects the trimester framework established in* Roe, *contend-
ing that states may enact regulations on abortion during all trimesters of pregnancy as long as such regulations do not constitute
an undue burden. She concludes that whereas regulations such as
Pennsylvania's twenty-four-hour waiting period and its parental
consent requirement do not pose an undue burden on women, a
spousal notification requirement is an undue burden. Sandra Day
O'Connor was the first female member of the US Supreme Court,
serving as associate justice from 1981 to 2006.*

Sandra Day O'Connor, Opinion of the Court, *Planned Parenthood of Southeastern
Pennsylvania v. Casey,* US Supreme Court, June 29, 1992.

L iberty finds no refuge in a jurisprudence of doubt. Yet 19 years after our holding that the Constitution protects a woman's right to terminate her pregnancy in its early stages, *Roe v. Wade* (1973), that definition of liberty is still questioned. . . .

The Essential Holding of *Roe*

It must be stated at the outset and with clarity that *Roe*'s essential holding, the holding we reaffirm, has three parts. First is a recognition of the right of the woman to choose to have an abortion before viability and to obtain it without undue interference from the State. Before viability, the State's interests are not strong enough to support a prohibition of abortion or the imposition of a substantial obstacle to the woman's effective right to elect the procedure. Second is a confirmation of the State's power to restrict abortions after fetal viability, if the law contains exceptions for pregnancies which endanger the woman's life or health. And third is the principle that the State has legitimate interests from the outset of the pregnancy in protecting the health of the woman and the life of the fetus that may become a child. These principles do not contradict one another; and we adhere to each. . . .

The woman's right to terminate her pregnancy before viability is the most central principle of *Roe v. Wade*. It is a rule of law and a component of liberty we cannot renounce.

On the other side of the equation is the interest of the State in the protection of potential life. The *Roe* Court recognized the State's "important and legitimate interest in protecting the potentiality of human life." The weight to be given this state interest, not the strength of the woman's interest, was the difficult question faced in *Roe*. We do not need to say whether each of us, had we been Members of the Court when the valuation of the state interest came before it as an original matter, would have concluded, as the *Roe* Court did, that its weight is insufficient to justify a ban on abortions prior to viability even when it is subject to certain exceptions. The matter is not before us in the first instance, and coming as it does after nearly 20 years of litigation in *Roe*'s wake

US SUPPORT FOR SPECIFIC ABORTION RESTRICTIONS

Do you favor or oppose each of the following proposals?

	Favor	Oppose
A law requiring doctors to inform patients about certain risks of abortion before performing the procedure	87%	11%
A law requiring women under 18 to get parental consent for any abortion	71%	27%
A law requiring women seeking abortions to wait 24 hours before having the procedure done	69%	28%
A law which would make it illegal to perform a specific abortion procedure conducted in the last six months of pregnancy known as a "partial birth abortion," except in cases necessary to save the life of the mother	64%	31%
A law requiring women seeking an abortion to be shown an ultrasound image of her fetus at least 24 hours before the procedure	50%	46%
A law allowing pharmacists and health providers to opt out of providing medicine or surgical procedures that result in abortion	46%	51%
A law prohibiting health clinics that provide abortion services from receiving any federal funds	40%	57%

Taken from: Gallup poll, July 15–17, 2011.

we are satisfied that the immediate question is not the soundness of *Roe*'s resolution of the issue, but the precedential force that must be accorded to its holding. And we have concluded that the essential holding of *Roe* should be reaffirmed.

Yet it must be remembered that *Roe v. Wade* speaks with clarity in establishing not only the woman's liberty but also the State's "important and legitimate interest in potential life." That portion of the decision in *Roe* has been given too little acknowledgment and implementation by the Court in its subsequent cases. Those cases decided that any regulation touching upon the abortion decision must survive strict scrutiny, to be sustained only if drawn in narrow terms to further a compelling state interest. Not all of the cases decided under that formulation can be reconciled with the holding in *Roe* itself that the State has legitimate interests in the health of the woman and in protecting the potential life within her. In resolving this tension, we choose to rely upon *Roe*, as against the later cases.

The Trimester Framework

Roe established a trimester framework to govern abortion regulations. Under this elaborate but rigid construct, almost no regulation at all is permitted during the first trimester of pregnancy; regulations designed to protect the woman's health, but not to further the State's interest in potential life, are permitted during the second trimester; and during the third trimester, when the fetus is viable, prohibitions are permitted provided the life or health of the mother is not at stake. Most of our cases since *Roe* have involved the application of rules derived from the trimester framework.

The trimester framework no doubt was erected to ensure that the woman's right to choose not become so subordinate to the State's interest in promoting fetal life that her choice exists in theory but not in fact. We do not agree, however, that the trimester approach is necessary to accomplish this objective. A framework of this rigidity was unnecessary and in its later interpretation sometimes contradicted the State's permissible exercise of its powers.

Though the woman has a right to choose to terminate or continue her pregnancy before viability, it does not at all follow that the State is prohibited from taking steps to ensure that this choice is thoughtful and informed. Even in the earliest stages of pregnancy, the State may enact rules and regulations designed to encourage her to know that there are philosophic and social arguments of great weight that can be brought to bear in favor of continuing the pregnancy to full term and that there are procedures and institutions to allow adoption of unwanted children as well as a certain degree of state assistance if the mother chooses to raise the child herself. "'[T]he Constitution does not forbid a State or city, pursuant to democratic processes, from expressing a preference for normal childbirth'" [*Webster v. Reproductive Health Services* (1989), quoting *Poelker v. Doe* (1977)]. It follows that States are free to enact laws to provide a reasonable framework for a woman to make a decision that has such profound and lasting meaning. This, too, we find consistent with *Roe's* central premises, and indeed the inevitable consequence of our holding that the State has an interest in protecting the life of the unborn.

We reject the trimester framework, which we do not consider to be part of the essential holding of *Roe*. Measures aimed at ensuring that a woman's choice contemplates the consequences for the fetus do not necessarily interfere with the right recognized in *Roe*, although those measures have been found to be inconsistent with the rigid trimester framework announced in that case. A logical reading of the central holding in *Roe* itself, and a necessary reconciliation of the liberty of the woman and the interest of the State in promoting prenatal life, require, in our view, that we abandon the trimester framework as a rigid prohibition on all previability regulation aimed at the protection of fetal life. The trimester framework suffers from these basic flaws: in its formulation it misconceives the nature of the pregnant woman's interest; and in practice it undervalues the State's interest in potential life, as recognized in *Roe.*

State Regulation of Abortion

As our jurisprudence relating to all liberties save perhaps abortion has recognized, not every law which makes a right more difficult to exercise is, *ipso facto* [by that very fact], an infringement of that right. An example clarifies the point. We have held that not every ballot access limitation amounts to an infringement of the right to vote. Rather, the States are granted substantial flexibility in establishing the framework within which voters choose the candidates for whom they wish to vote.

The abortion right is similar. Numerous forms of state regulation might have the incidental effect of increasing the cost or decreasing the availability of medical care, whether for abortion or any other medical procedure. The fact that a law which serves a valid purpose, one not designed to strike at the right itself, has the incidental effect of making it more difficult or more expensive to procure an abortion cannot be enough to invalidate it. Only where state regulation imposes an undue burden on a woman's ability to make this decision does the power of the State reach into the heart of the liberty protected by the Due Process Clause.

For the most part, the Court's early abortion cases adhered to this view. In *Maher v. Roe* (1977), the Court explained: "*Roe* did not declare an unqualified 'constitutional right to an abortion,' as the District Court seemed to think. Rather, the right protects the woman from unduly burdensome interference with her freedom to decide whether to terminate her pregnancy."

These considerations of the nature of the abortion right illustrate that it is an overstatement to describe it as a right to decide whether to have an abortion "without interference from the State" [*Planned Parenthood of Central Missouri v. Danforth* (1976)]. All abortion regulations interfere to some degree with a woman's ability to decide whether to terminate her pregnancy. It is, as a consequence, not surprising that despite the protestations contained in the original *Roe* opinion to the effect that the Court was not recognizing an absolute right, the Court's experience applying the trimester framework has led to the striking down of some abortion regulations which in no real sense deprived women of the ultimate decision. Those decisions went too far because the right recognized by *Roe* is a right "to be free from unwarranted governmental intrusion into matters so fundamentally affecting a person as the decision whether to bear or beget a child," [*Eisenstadt v. Baird* (1972)]. Not all governmental intrusion is of necessity unwarranted; and that brings us to the other basic flaw in the trimester framework: even in *Roe*'s terms, in practice it undervalues the State's interest in the potential life within the woman.

Roe v. Wade was express in its recognition of the State's "important and legitimate interest[s] in preserving and protecting the health of the pregnant woman [and] in protecting the potentiality of human life." The trimester framework, however, does not fulfill *Roe*'s own promise that the State has an interest in protecting fetal life or potential life. *Roe* began the contradiction by using the trimester framework to forbid any regulation of abortion designed to advance that interest before viability. Before viability, *Roe* and subsequent cases treat all governmental attempts to influence a woman's decision on behalf of the potential life within her as unwarranted. This treatment is, in our judgment, incompatible with the recognition that there is a substantial state interest in potential life throughout pregnancy.

The Undue Burden Standard

The very notion that the State has a substantial interest in potential life leads to the conclusion that not all regulations must be deemed unwarranted. Not all burdens on the right to decide whether to terminate a pregnancy will be undue. In our view, the undue burden standard is the appropriate means of reconciling the State's interest with the woman's constitutionally protected liberty.

US Supreme Court justice Sandra Day O'Connor, the first woman to serve on the high court, wrote the 1992 decision rejecting Roe's trimester framework. © AP Images.

The concept of an undue burden has been utilized by the Court as well as individual Members of the Court, including two of us, in ways that could be considered inconsistent. Because we set forth a standard of general application to which we intend to adhere, it is important to clarify what is meant by an undue burden.

A finding of an undue burden is a shorthand for the conclusion that a state regulation has the purpose or effect of placing a substantial obstacle in the path of a woman seeking an abortion of a nonviable fetus. A statute with this purpose is invalid because the means chosen by the State to further the interest in potential life must be calculated to inform the woman's free choice, not hinder it. And a statute which, while furthering the interest in potential life or some other valid state interest, has the effect of placing a substantial obstacle in the path of a woman's choice cannot be considered a permissible means of serving its legitimate ends. To the extent that the opinions of the Court or of individual Justices use the undue burden standard in a manner that is inconsistent with this analysis, we set out what in our view should be the controlling standard. In our considered judgment, an undue burden is an unconstitutional burden. Understood another way, we answer the question, left open in previous opinions discussing the undue burden formulation, whether a law designed to further the State's interest in fetal life which imposes an undue burden on the woman's decision before fetal viability could be constitutional. The answer is no.

Some guiding principles should emerge. What is at stake is the woman's right to make the ultimate decision, not a right to be insulated from all others in doing so. Regulations which do no more than create a structural mechanism by which the State, or the parent or guardian of a minor, may express profound respect for the life of the unborn are permitted, if they are not a substantial obstacle to the woman's exercise of the right to choose. Unless it has that effect on her right of choice, a state measure designed to persuade her to choose childbirth over abortion will be upheld if reasonably related to that goal. Regulations designed to foster the health of a woman seeking an abortion are valid if they do not constitute an undue burden. . . .

Pennsylvania's Abortion Regulations

Our analysis of Pennsylvania's 24-hour waiting period between the provision of the information deemed necessary to informed consent and the performance of an abortion under the undue burden standard requires us to reconsider the premise behind the decision in *Akron I* [*Akron v. Akron Center for Reproductive Health, Inc.* (1983)] invalidating a parallel requirement. In *Akron I* we said: "Nor are we convinced that the State's legitimate concern that the woman's decision be informed is reasonably served by requiring a 24-hour delay as a matter of course." We consider that conclusion to be wrong. The idea that important decisions will be more informed and deliberate if they follow some period of reflection does not strike us as unreasonable, particularly where the statute directs that important information become part of the background of the decision. The statute, as construed by the Court of Appeals, permits avoidance of the waiting period in the event of a medical emergency and the record evidence shows that in the vast majority of cases, a 24-hour delay does not create any appreciable health risk. In theory, at least, the waiting period is a reasonable measure to implement the State's interest in protecting the life of the unborn, a measure that does not amount to an undue burden. . . .

Section 3209 of Pennsylvania's abortion law provides, except in cases of medical emergency, that no physician shall perform an abortion on a married woman without receiving a signed statement from the woman that she has notified her spouse that she is about to undergo an abortion. . . .

In well-functioning marriages, spouses discuss important intimate decisions such as whether to bear a child. But there are millions of women in this country who are the victims of regular physical and psychological abuse at the hands of their husbands.

Should these women become pregnant, they may have very good reasons for not wishing to inform their husbands of their decision to obtain an abortion. Many may have justifiable fears of physical abuse, but may be no less fearful of the consequences of reporting prior abuse to the Commonwealth of Pennsylvania. Many may have a reasonable fear that notifying their husbands will provoke further instances of child abuse; these women are not exempt from § 3209's notification requirement. Many may fear devastating forms of psychological abuse from their husbands, including verbal harassment, threats of future violence, the destruction of possessions, physical confinement to the home, the withdrawal of financial support, or the disclosure of the abortion to family and friends. These methods of psychological abuse may act as even more of a deterrent to notification than the possibility of physical violence, but women who are the victims of the abuse are not exempt from § 3209's notification requirement. And many women who are pregnant as a result of sexual assaults by their husbands will be unable to avail themselves of the exception for spousal sexual assault, § 3209(b)(3), because the exception requires that the woman have notified law enforcement authorities within 90 days of the assault, and her husband will be notified of her report once an investigation begins, § 3128(e). If anything in this field is certain, it is that victims of spousal sexual assault are extremely reluctant to report the abuse to the government; hence, a great many spousal rape victims will not be exempt from the notification requirement imposed by § 3209.

The spousal notification requirement is thus likely to prevent a significant number of women from obtaining an abortion. It does not merely make abortions a little more difficult or expensive to obtain; for many women, it will impose a substantial obstacle. We must not blind ourselves to the fact that the significant number of women who fear for their safety and the safety of their children are likely to be deterred from procuring an abortion as surely as if the Commonwealth had outlawed abortion in all cases. . . .

It is an undue burden, and therefore invalid.

This conclusion is in no way inconsistent with our decisions upholding parental notification or consent requirements. . . .

Except in a medical emergency, an unemancipated young woman under 18 may not obtain an abortion unless she and one of her parents (or guardian) provide informed consent. . . . If neither a parent nor a guardian provides consent, a court may authorize the performance of an abortion upon a determination that the young woman is mature and capable of giving informed consent and has in fact given her informed consent, or that an abortion would be in her best interests.

We have been over most of this ground before. Our cases establish, and we reaffirm today, that a State may require a minor seeking an abortion to obtain the consent of a parent or guardian, provided that there is an adequate judicial bypass procedure.

> *"Parental involvement laws protect the health and welfare of minors, as well as foster family unity and protect the constitutional rights of parents to rear their children."*

Parental Involvement Laws for Abortion Protect Minors

Mailee R. Smith

In the following viewpoint, a lawyer argues that parental involvement laws in abortion—including parental notification laws and parental consent laws—protect minors and parents. The author contends that current parental notification laws could benefit from better enforcement and more stringent requirements. Furthermore, she argues that clarification is needed for courts in assessing a minor's maturity level, should a minor use the courts to attempt to bypass the parental involvement requirement. She claims that there are many myths about parental involvement laws, and she denies that the laws pose a danger to minors, as some have charged. Mailee R. Smith is staff counsel for Americans United for Life, a nonprofit pro-life law and policy organization.

Thirteen-year-old "Jane Doe" was your everyday teen: She attended school and played on the school soccer team. But her normal life turned into a nightmare when her soccer coach initiated a sexual relationship with her, impregnated her, and took her to a local Ohio Planned Parenthood clinic for an abortion. The clinic never questioned the soccer coach, who posed over the phone as Jane's father and then personally paid for the girl's abortion. And where were her real parents? Their consent was never sought. In fact, they were never even informed.

Sadly, Jane's story is not unique. Almost daily news stories reveal yet another teen that has been sexually abused by a person in authority—a coach, teacher, or other authority figure. Daily, teens are taken to abortion clinics without the consent or even the knowledge of their parents. The health and welfare of these minors is at risk, especially in states where parental involvement laws have not been enacted.

Parental Involvement Laws

In 1992, a plurality of the U.S. Supreme Court ruled that a state may constitutionally require a minor seeking an abortion to obtain the consent of a parent or guardian. Specifically, the Court held that certain provisions, such as a required reflection period and a chance for parents to privately discuss with their daughters the values and moral principles of the situation, carry particular force with respect to minors. Based upon the Court's decision and subsequent lower federal court decisions, a parental involvement law is constitutional and does not place an undue burden on minors if it contains the following provisions:

- For consent, no physician may perform an abortion upon a minor or incompetent person unless the physician has the consent of one parent or legal guardian. For notice, no physician may perform an abortion upon a minor or incompetent person unless the physician performing the abortion has given 48 hours notice to a parent or legal guardian of the minor or incompetent person.

- An exception to the consent or notice requirement exists when there is a medical emergency or when notice is waived by the person entitled to receive the notice.
- A minor may bypass the requirement through the courts (*i.e.*, judicial bypass).

The purpose behind parental involvement laws is clear. Immature minors often lack the ability to make fully informed choices that take into account both immediate and long-range consequences. Yet the medical, emotional, and psychological consequences of abortion are often serious and can be lasting, particularly when the patient is immature. Moreover, parents usually possess information essential to a physician's exercise of his or her best medical judgment concerning the minor. Parents who are aware that their minor has had an abortion may better ensure the best post-abortion medical attention. As such, parental consultation is usually desirable and in the best interest of the minor. For these reasons, parental involvement laws protect the health and welfare of minors, as well as foster family unity and protect the constitutional rights of parents to rear their children.

AUL [Americans United for Life] has drafted both a "Parental Consent for Abortion Act" as well as a "Parental Notification of Abortion Act."

Proposed Enhancements to Parental Involvement Laws

The situation surrounding Jane Doe's abortion may have been different if the local Planned Parenthood affiliate had followed the law in Ohio. Unfortunately, it is often too easy for abortion clinics to sidestep the law by claiming they were duped into believing they had contacted the proper party. A simple way to combat such claims is to reinforce current parental involvement laws with identification or notarization requirements.

More specifically, states should require that parents present positive, government-issued identification before a minor ob-

The Importance of Medical and Health Information

Parental involvement statutes provide parents the opportunity to supply the abortion provider with the minor's medical and health information, as well as an opportunity for the parents to discuss and arrange adequate post-abortion care. Without these opportunities for parent-physician consultation and cooperation, the health of minors is put at serious risk. An abortion provider should know the medical history and background of the woman seeking an abortion, to make the best medical judgment regarding whether or not an abortion would be in the best interests of the woman.

Maggie Datiles, "Parental Involvement Laws for Abortion: Protecting both Minors and Their Parents," Culture of Life Foundation, April 18, 2008. www.culture-of-life.org.

tains an abortion. A step further would require that parents' consent forms are notarized. Copies of the identification or notarized documents must then be kept by the abortion clinic in the minors' medical records. When such actions are required, ignorance of an adult's true identity is no excuse for failing to follow the law.

Another way to enhance existing parental involvement laws is to enact specific standards for judicial review in evaluating judicial bypass petitions. Currently, most consent and notice requirements contain very basic criteria, simply requiring that the minor be mature enough to make the decision, or requiring that the abortion would be in the minor's "best interest."

An Arizona appellate court case has delineated the type of criteria a judge should use in evaluating the maturity of a minor petitioning for judicial bypass. It is an excellent example of how the more basic judicial bypass requirements can be enhanced.

Anti-abortion activists protest in front of the US Supreme Court building in Washington, DC. Pro-life advocates argue that parental consent requirements for abortion protect minors. © Chris Maddaloni/Roll Call/Getty Images.

Looking to U.S. Supreme Court precedent stating that minors "often lack the experience, perspective, and judgment to recognize and avoid choices that could be detrimental to them" [*Bellotti v. Baird* (1979)], the court concluded that maturity may be measured by examining a minor's experience, perspective, and judgment.

"Experience" refers to all that has happened to the minor during her lifetime, including the things she has seen or done. Examples include the minor's age and experiences working outside the home, living away from home, traveling on her own, handling her personal finances, and making other significant decisions.

"Perspective" refers to the minor's ability to appreciate and understand the relative gravity and possible detrimental impact of available options, as well as the potential consequences of each. Specific examples include the steps she took to explore her options and the extent to which she considered and weighed the potential consequences of abortion.

"Judgment" refers to the minor's intellectual and emotional ability to make the abortion decision without the consent of her parents or guardian. This includes the minor's conduct since learning of her pregnancy and her intellectual ability to understand her options and make an informed decision. Consideration should be given to whether the minor's decision resulted from impulse rather than careful consideration.

Such guidelines will give judges the foundation they need to more freely evaluate the true maturity level of those minors seeking an abortion without parental involvement. . . .

Myths and Facts About Parental Involvement Laws

Myth: An estimated 12 percent of teens do not even live with their parents. Involving the parents of these teens will be impossible and totally unrelated to the teen's health.

Fact: Parental involvement legislation recognizes that many family situations are less than ideal. In most states, alternative procedures are available through judicial bypass, and some states allow notification or consent of another family member.

Myth: Mandatory parental involvement laws will force many teens to go out of state to obtain an abortion.

Fact: As more states enact and enforce parental involvement laws, the option to go out of state will cease to exist, and parental rights and minors' health protection will continue to expand. Migration to other states is a reason to pass parental involvement laws, not to avoid them.

Myth: Parental involvement laws simply delay teens from getting abortions until the second trimester, when abortion is more dangerous.

Fact: This myth is directly contrary to data from both Minnesota and Missouri.

Myth: Parental involvement laws force teens to obtain dangerous illegal abortions.

Fact: The majority of states have enforceable parental involvement laws. Only one case—that of Becky Bell in Indiana—has been suggested to involve an unsafe abortion, and even that case is wholly undocumented. The autopsy report failed to show any induced abortion. It is terrible public policy to fail to enact a law on the basis of an isolated, unproven case.

Myth: Parental involvement laws expose teens to the anger of abusive parents.

Fact: Under the parental involvement laws in most states, a teen who states she has been abused or neglected will be exempted from the laws' requirements. In addition, the laws make it more likely that a minor who is being abused or neglected will get the help she needs; under most state laws, doctors who become aware of abuse claims must report the abuse allegation to public officials who conduct an anonymous investigation. Such teens also have the option of utilizing the judicial bypass procedure.

Myth: Most teens are mature enough to make their own decisions.

Fact: Young teens often have difficulty assessing long-term consequences and generally have narrow and egocentric views of their problems. Parental involvement is needed to give teenagers some perspective. Moreover, the question is not simply of maturity, but of responsibility. As long as a teenager is not emancipated, a parent or guardian is responsible for her medical care and upbringing. When a teen is injured by an abortion, it is the parent or guardian—not the teen—who is responsible for the teen's care and health costs.

*"Mandatory parental-involvement
(consent and notice) laws do not solve
the problem of inadequate family
communication; they only exacerbate a
potentially dangerous situation."*

Mandatory Parental-Involvement Laws Threaten Young Women's Safety

NARAL Pro-Choice America

*In the following viewpoint, a pro-choice advocacy organization
argues that state laws that require parental notice or parental consent prior to allowing a minor to get an abortion endanger the
health and well-being of young women. The organization contends
that the government cannot mandate healthy family communication and parental involvement laws put minors at risk emotionally,
physically, and medically. The organization denies that the judicial
bypass alternative for granting consent alleviates the dangers and
concludes that all parental involvement laws should be eliminated.
NARAL Pro-Choice America is an advocacy organization working
to protect a woman's right to choose abortion.*

There are two types of parental-involvement laws; those
that require parental *notice* and those that require parental

consent before a minor can seek abortion services. Parental-notice laws require prior written notification of parents before an abortion can be performed, with limited exceptions, such as in cases of physical abuse, incest, or medical emergency. These laws also may prescribe other preconditions including a mandatory waiting period following the parents' receipt of notification, and/or judicial intervention if there are compelling reasons to avoid parental notification.

Parental-consent laws require that minors obtain the consent of one or both parents before they can receive abortion services. As is the case with parental notice, a judicial-bypass process is also included in parental-consent laws. The penalties for violating parental-consent laws range from civil liability and fines to imprisonment. The Supreme Court has ruled that parental-consent requirements are constitutional so long as they include a judicial-bypass procedure to accommodate those young women who cannot involve their parents.

Ideally, a teen facing a crisis will seek the advice and counsel of those who care for her most and know her best. In fact, even in the absence of laws mandating parental involvement, many young women do turn to their parents when they are considering abortion. Unfortunately, some young women cannot involve their parents because physical violence or emotional abuse is present in their homes, because their pregnancies are the result of incest, or because they fear parental anger and disappointment. Mandatory parental-involvement (consent and notice) laws do not solve the problem of inadequate family communication; they only exacerbate a potentially dangerous situation.

In some circumstances, teens facing an unintended pregnancy feel compelled to travel to another state where there is a less stringent parental-involvement law or no such law at all to avoid involving their parents and maintain their privacy. In the most dire of circumstances, some pregnant young women who fear telling their parents may resort to illegal or self-induced abortions that may result in death. Yet, despite these severe consequences, 38 states currently enforce laws that require a minor to obtain the consent of, or notify, an adult—typically a parent—prior to an abortion.[1] And five other states have minors' access laws that are either enjoined or not enforced.[2]

In recent years, anti-choice legislators in Congress have attempted to pass two pieces of federal legislation that would impose draconian criminal parental-involvement laws on every state in the country. The first, called the "Child Custody Protection Act," criminalizes caring and loving adults—including grandparents, adult siblings, and religious counselors—who accompany a teen out of state for abortion care if the home state parental-involvement law has not been met.[3] The second, called the "Child Interstate Abortion Notification Act," in addition to the restrictive provisions in the CCPA, also would impose a convoluted patchwork of parental-involvement laws on women and doctors across the country, making it virtually impossible for young women to access abortion services in another state.[4] Both measures would threaten young women's health and deny them the support and guidance they need from responsible and caring adults.

Government Cannot Mandate Healthy and Open Communications in Families

Government cannot mandate healthy family communication. Laws requiring parental notice or consent actually may endanger the young women they purport to protect by increasing the possibility of illegal and self-induced abortion, family violence, suicide, later abortions, and unwanted childbirth.[5]

- A majority of young adults who are pregnant and seek abortion care indicate that their parents are aware that they are doing so.[6] Furthermore, in states without parental-involvement laws, 61 percent of parents knew of their daughter's decision to terminate a pregnancy.[7]

Nancy Keenan, the president of NARAL Pro-Choice America, speaks at an event commemorating the thirty-eighth anniversary of Roe v. Wade *in 2011.* © Kris Connor/Getty Images Entertainment/Getty Images.

- Even before reaching the point of having to discuss abortion, research indicates that a majority of teens talk to their parents about sex, STDs, and birth control.[8]
- The American Medical Association takes the position that: "Physicians should not feel or be compelled to require minors to involve their parents before deciding whether to undergo an abortion. . . . [M]inors should ultimately be allowed to decide whether parental involvement is appropriate."[9]
- The American Academy of Pediatrics also opposes parental-involvement laws: "Legislation mandating parental involvement does not achieve the intended benefit of promoting family communication but it does increase the risk of harm to the adolescent by delaying access to appropriate medical care. . . . [M]inors should not be compelled or required to involve their parents in their decisions to obtain abortions, although they should be encouraged to discuss their pregnancies with their parents and other responsible adults."[10]
- Parental-involvement laws appear to have had little effect on reducing abortion rates among teens.[11]

Many Young Women Who Do Not Involve a Parent Have Good Reasons

Most young women find love, support, and safety in their home. Many, however, justifiably fear that they would be physically or emotionally abused if forced to disclose their pregnancy. Often, young women who do not involve a parent come from families where government-mandated disclosure would have devastating effects.

- An estimated 772,000 children were found to be victims of abuse or neglect in 2008.[12] Young women considering abortion are particularly vulnerable because research shows that family violence is often at its worst during a family member's pregnancy.[13]

- Nearly half of pregnant teens who have a history of abuse report being assaulted during their pregnancy, most often by a family member.[14] As the Supreme Court has recognized, "Mere notification of pregnancy is frequently a flashpoint for battering and violence within the family. The number of battering incidents is high during the pregnancy and often the worst abuse can be associated with pregnancy."[15]

- Among minors who did not tell a parent of their abortion, 30 percent had experienced violence in their family or feared violence or being forced to leave home.[16] "My older sister got pregnant when she was seventeen. My mother pushed her against the wall, slapped her across the face and then grabbed her by the hair, pulled her through the living room out the front door and threw her off the porch. We don't know where she is now."[17]

- In Idaho, a 13-year-old student named Spring Adams was shot to death by her father after he learned she was to terminate a pregnancy caused by his acts of incest.[18]

Mandatory Parental-Consent and Notice Laws Endanger Young Women's Health

Parental-consent and notice laws endanger young women's health by forcing some women—even some from healthy, loving families—to turn to illegal or self-induced abortion, delay the procedure and increase the medical risk, or bear a child against their will.

- In Indiana, Rebecca Bell, a young woman who had a very close relationship with her parents, died from an illegal abortion that she sought because she did not want her parents to know about her pregnancy. Indiana law required parental consent before she could have a legal abortion.[19]

- The American Medical Association has noted that "[b]ecause the need for privacy may be compelling, minors may be driven to desperate measures to maintain the confidentiality of their pregnancies. They may run away from home, obtain a 'back alley' abortion, or resort to self-induced abortion. The desire to maintain secrecy has been one of the leading reasons for illegal abortion deaths since . . . 1973."[20]

- Recognizing that maintaining confidentiality is essential to minors' willingness to obtain necessary health care related to sexual activity, all 50 states and the District of Columbia authorize minors to consent to the diagnosis and treatment of sexually transmitted infections without parental consent.[21] Many states explicitly include testing and treatment of HIV, with only one state requiring parental notification if a minor tests positive for HIV.[22] In addition, the Supreme Court has recognized that confidential access to contraceptives is essential for minors to exercise their constitutional right to privacy,[23] and federal law requires confidentiality for minors receiving family-planning services through publicly funded programs, such as Title X and Medicaid.[24]

- According to Leslie Tarr Laurie, president of Tapestry Health Systems, a Massachusetts-based health services provider: "Confidentiality is the cornerstone of our services. . . . We help teenagers avoid not only the costly and often tragic consequences of unintended pregnancy and childbearing, but also an early death from AIDS. The bottom line is, if we don't assure access to confidential health care, teenagers simply will stop seeking the care they desire and need."[25]

Judicial-Bypass Provisions Fail to Protect Young Women

In challenges to two different parental-involvement laws, the Supreme Court has ruled that a state statute requiring parental involvement must have some sort of bypass procedure, such as a judicial bypass, in order to be constitutional[26] and that no one person may have an absolute veto over a minor's decision to have

Abortion

STATES WITH PARENTAL INVOLVEMENT LAWS, MARCH 2012

State	Parental Involvement		
	Consent Only	Notification and Consent	Notification Only
Alabama	X	---	---
Alaska	---	---	X
Arizona	X✪	---	---
Arkansas	X✪	---	---
California	▼	---	---
Colorado	---	---	X
Delaware	---	---	X+◇
Florida	---	---	X
Georgia	---	---	X
Idaho	X	---	---
Illinois	---	---	△
Indiana	X	---	---
Iowa	---	---	X
Kansas	Both parents✪	---	---
Kentucky	X	---	---
Louisiana	X✪	---	---
Maryland	---	---	X+
Massachusetts	X	---	---
Michigan	X	---	---
Minnesota	---	---	Both parents
Mississippi	Both parents	---	---
Missouri	X	---	---
Montana	---	---	▼
Nebraska	X✪	---	---
Nevada	---	---	▼

Taken from: Guttmacher Institute, "Parental Involvement in Minor' Abortions," *State Policies in Brief*, March 1, 2012.

STATES WITH PARENTAL INVOLVEMENT LAWS, MARCH 2012 (continued)

State	Parental Involvement		
	Consent Only	Notification and Consent	Notification Only
New Hampshire	---	---	X
New Jersey	---	---	▼
New Mexico	▼	---	---
North Carolina	X	---	---
North Dakota	Both parents	---	---
Ohio	X	---	---
Oklahoma	---	X	---
Pennsylvania	X	---	---
Rhode Island	X	---	---
South Carolina	X✚◇	---	---
South Dakota	---	---	X
Tennessee	X	---	---
Texas	---	X✪	---
Utah	---	X	---
Virginia	---	X✪	---
West Virginia	---	---	X✚
Wisconsin	X✚	---	---
Wyoming	---	X	---

▼ Enforcement permanently enjoined by court order; policy not in effect.

△ Enforcement temporarily enjoined by court order; policy not in effect.

✪ Requires parental consent documentation to be notarized.

✚ Allows specified health professionals to waive parental involvement in limited circumstances.

◇ While most state laws apply to all minors, Delaware's law applies to women younger than 16 and South Carolina's law applies to those younger than 17.

an abortion.[27] Thus, most states that require parental consent or notice provide—at least as a matter of law—a judicial bypass through which a young woman can seek a court order allowing an abortion without parental involvement.

But bypass procedures are often an inadequate alternative for young women, especially when courts are either not equipped or resistant to granting judicial bypasses. Even for adults, going to court for a judicial order is difficult. For young women without a lawyer, it is overwhelming and at times impossible. Some young women cannot maneuver the legal procedures required or cannot attend hearings scheduled during school hours. Others do not go or delay going because they fear that the proceedings are not confidential or that they will be recognized by people at the courthouse. Many experience fear and distress and do not want to reveal intimate details of their personal lives to strangers.[28] The time required to schedule the court proceeding may result in a delay of a week or more, thereby increasing the health risks of the abortion.[29] And in many instances, courts are not equipped to handle bypass proceedings in accord with constitutional regulations.[30] Worse yet, some young women who do manage to arrange a hearing face judges who are vehemently anti-choice and who routinely deny petitions of minors who show that they are mature or that the bypass is in their best interest, despite rulings by the U.S. Supreme Court that the bypass must be granted in those circumstances.[31]

- In denying the petition of one young woman, a Missouri judge stated: "Depending upon what ruling I make I hold in my hands the power to kill an unborn child. In our society it's a lot easier to kill an unborn child than the most vicious murderer. . . . I don't believe that this particular juvenile has sufficient intellectual capacity to make a determination that she is willing to kill her own child."[32]
- A Toledo, Ohio judge denied a bypass for a 17-year-old, an "A" student who planned to attend college and who testified

she was not financially or emotionally prepared for college and motherhood at the same time, stating that the girl had "not had enough hard knocks in her life."[33]

- In Louisiana, a judge denied a 15-year-old a bypass petition after asking her a series of inappropriate questions, including what the minor would say to the fetus about her decision. Her request was granted only after a rehearing by six appellate court judges.[34]

- A Pennsylvania study found that of the 60 judicial districts in the state, only eight were able to provide complete information about Pennsylvania's judicial-bypass procedure. Some county courts referred minors to anti-choice crisis pregnancy centers that typically provide false and misleading information about abortion and pressure women to carry their pregnancies to term.[35]

- The Alabama Supreme Court upheld a trial court's denial of a petition for a 17-year-old because the minor's testimony appeared "rehearsed" and she did not show "any emotion." The trial court refused to find that the minor was mature and well-informed enough to make her own decision or that an abortion was in her best interests—despite the fact that the 17-year-old high school senior had a 3.0 grade point average, had been accepted to college, had discussed her options with the father of the fetus, had spoken to a doctor, a counselor, her godmother, and her 20-year-old sister, was able to describe the abortion procedure, was informed about its risks, and had testified that her legal guardian had thrown a teenage relative out of the house when she became pregnant.[36]

The Effects of Teenage Childbearing Can Be Devastating

The forced childbearing among teenagers that can result from parental-consent and notice laws can have devastating effects on the health and life chances of young women and their children.

- Approximately one-third of American women become pregnant before the age of 20.[37]
- Fewer than 60 percent of teen mothers graduate from high school by age 25—compared to 90 percent of those who postpone childbearing.[38] Furthermore, more than half of Hispanic teen mothers do not complete high school.[39]
- Teens that give birth spend a greater length of time receiving public assistance—an average of three years longer than older mothers through age 35.[40]
- Approximately one-quarter of teen mothers go on welfare within three years of the child's birth.[41] Teen mothers are also more likely to have lower family incomes later in life.[42]
- Infants of teen mothers are one-third more likely to suffer from low birth weight (less than 5.5 pounds) than those born to older mothers.[43] The children of teenage parents have an increased risk of abuse and neglect and are more likely to become teenage parents themselves, thus perpetuating the cycle of poverty.[44]
- Teen mothers are likely to have a second child relatively soon after their first—about a quarter of teen mothers have a second child within 24 months of the first. This can further inhibit their ability to finish school, keep a job, and escape poverty.[45]

Making Abortion Less Necessary Among Teenagers Requires a Comprehensive Effort to Prevent Teen Pregnancy

Abortion among teenagers should be made less necessary, not more difficult and dangerous. A comprehensive approach to promoting adolescent reproductive health and reducing teen pregnancy will require an array of components, including:

- age-appropriate, comprehensive sex education with medically accurate information;

- access to confidential health services, including family planning;
- life-options programs that offer young people practical life skills and the motivation to delay sexual activity; and
- programs for pregnant and parenting teens that teach parenting skills and help ensure that teens finish school.
- Access to pre natal care and comprehensive health-care coverage.

Such an approach has never been implemented on a significant scale in the United States, and several studies of specific HIV-prevention and sex education programs demonstrate positive outcomes such as increased knowledge, delay in onset of sex, reduction in the frequency of sex, or increased contraceptive use.[46] The wisest policy gives teenagers the tools they need to avoid pregnancy and forsakes misguided efforts to insert the government into delicate family situations.

Notes

1. The 38 states with enforceable mandatory consent and notice laws are: AK, AL, AZ, AR, CO, DE, FL, GA, ID, IN, IL, IA, KS, KY, LA, ME, MD, MA, MI, MN, MS, MO, NE, NC, ND, OH, OK, PA, RI, SC, SD, TN, TX, UT, VA, WV, WI, WY. NARAL Pro-Choice America Foundation, *Who Decides? The Status of Women's Reproductive Rights in the United States* (20th ed. 2011), available at www.WhoDecides.org.
2. The five states with laws that are either enjoined or not enforced are: CA, MT, NV, NJ, NM. NARAL Pro-Choice America & NARAL Pro-Choice America Foundation, *Who Decides? The Status of Women's Reproductive Rights in the United States* (20th ed. 2011), available at www.WhoDecides.org.
3. H.R.3682, 105th Cong. (1998); H.R.1218, 106th Cong. (1999); 145 Cong. Rec. H5122–23 (1999); 148 Cong. Rec. H (2002); S.661, 106th Cong. (1999); H.R.476, 107th Cong (2002); S.403, 109th Cong. (2006); S.2543, 110th Cong. (2008); S.1179, 111th Cong. (2009).
4. H.R.748, 109th Cong. (2006); S.403, 109th Cong. (2006); H.R.1063, 110th Cong. (2007); H.R. 634, 111th Cong. (2009).
5. Center for Reproductive Rights, *Parental Involvement Laws* (Jan. 14, 2009), at http:// reproductiverights.org/en/project/parental-involvement-laws (last visited Oct. 28, 2010).
6. Dennis, Amanda, Stanley K. Henshaw, Theodore J. Joyce, Lawrence B. Finer, & Kelly Blanchard. The Guttmacher Institute, *The Impact of Laws Requiring Parental Involvement for Abortion: A Literature Review* at page 3 (March 2009).

7. Martin Donohoe, *Parental Notification and Consent Laws for Teen Abortions: Overview and 2006 Ballot Measures*, MEDSCAPE Ob/Gyn & Women's Health, February 9, 2007 at http://www.medscape.com/viewarticle/549316 (last visited October 20, 2010).

8. Gladys Martinez, Ph.D, Joyce Abma, Ph.D., and Casey Copen, Ph.D. *Educating Teenagers About Sex in the United States*, U.S. Department of Health and Human Services; Centers for Disease Control and Prevention; National Center For Health Statistics, September 2010.

9. American Medical Association, Council on Ethical and Judicial Affairs, *Mandatory Parental Consent to Abortion*, Code of Medical Ethics 1996–1997 Edition, § 2.015 (issued June 1994) (based on the report, *Mandatory Parental Consent to Abortion* (issued June 1992) 269 JAMA 82–86 (1993)).

10. American Academy of Pediatrics, Committee on Adolescence, *The Adolescent's Right to Confidential Care When Considering Abortion*, 97 Pediatrics 746 (1996).

11. Dennis, Amanda, Stanley K. Henshaw, Theodore J. Joyce, Lawrence B. Finer, & Kelly Blanchard. The Guttmacher Institute, *The Impact of Laws Requiring Parental Involvement for Abortion: A Literature Review* at page 3 (March 2009); Virginia G. Cartoof & Lorraine V. Klerman, *Parental Consent for Abortion: Impact of the Massachusetts Law*, 76 American J. of Pub. Health 397–400 (1986); Stanley K. Henshaw, *The Impact of Requirement of Parental Consent on Minors' Abortions in Mississippi*, 27 Family Planning Perspectives 120–121 (1995). But see Theodore Joyce, Robert Kaestner, & Silvie Colman, *Changes in Abortions and Births and the Texas Parental Notification Law*, 354 New Eng. J. Med., 1031 (2006).

12. U.S. Department of Health and Human Services, Administration of Children, Youth and Families, Children's Bureau, *Child Maltreatment* 2008 (2010).

13. H. Amaro et al., *Violence During Pregnancy and Substance Abuse*, 80 American J. of Pub. Health 575–579 (1990); University of Pittsburg Medical Center, Information for Patients, Abuse During Pregnancy, ED/JAW Rev. (March 2003).

14. American Psychological Association, *Parental Consent Laws for Adolescent Reproductive Health Care: What Does the Psychological Research Say?* (Feb. 2000), citing A.B. Berenson, et al., *Prevalence of Physical and Sexual Assault in Pregnant Adolescents*, 13 J. of Adolescent Health 466–69 (1992).

15. *Planned Parenthood of Southeastern Pennsylvania v. Casey*, 505 U.S. 833, 889 (1992) (citing expert witness testimony).

16. Martin Donohoe, *Parental Notification and Consent Laws for Teen Abortions: Overview and 2006 Ballot Measures*, MEDSCAPE Ob/Gyn & Women's Health, February 9, 2007 at http://www.medscape.com/viewarticle/549316 (last visited October 20, 2010); Stanley K. Henshaw & Kathryn Kost, *Parental Involvement in Minors' Abortion Decisions*, 24 Family Planning Perspectives 197, 199–200 (1992).

17. Helena Silverstein, "Girls on the Stand: How Courts Fail Pregnant Minors (2007)," quoting Melissa Jacobs, "Are Courts Prepared to Handle Judicial Bypass Proceedings?" *Human Rights* 32 (Winter 2005): 4.

18. Margie Boule, *An American Tragedy*, Sunday Oregonian, August 27, 1989.

19. Rochelle Sharpe, *Abortion Law: Fatal Effect*, Gannett News Service, December 1, 1989; *60 Minutes*, (CBS television broadcast, February 24, 1991) (videotape on file with NARAL Pro-Choice America).

20. Council on Ethical and Judicial Affairs American Medical Association, *Mandatory Parental Consent to Abortion*, 269 JAMA 83 (1993).

21. The Alan Guttmacher Institute, *Minors' Access to STD Services*, State Policies in Brief, October 1, 2008.

22. The Alan Guttmacher Institute, *Minors' Access to STD Services*, State Policies in Brief, October 1, 2008.

23. *Carey v. Population Services International*, 431 U.S. 678 (1977).

24. *New York v. Heckler*, 719 F.2d 1191 (S.D.N.Y. 1983) (striking down regulation requiring parental notification within 10 days of a Title X-funded family planning center providing prescription drugs or devices to unemancipated minor because such law conflicted with the program requirements of Title X); *Planned Parenthood Association of Utah v. Dandoy*, 810 F.2d 984 (10th Cir. 1987) (holding state law requiring parental consent for Medicaid conflicted with federal law, which requires states participating in the Medicaid program to provide family planning assistance to eligible minors without parental involvement).

25. Heather Boonstra and Elizabeth Nash, *Minors and the Right to Consent to Health Care*, 3 The Guttmacher Report on Public Policy 8 (2000).

26. *Hodgson v. Minnesota*, 497 U.S. 417, 420 (1990) (requiring a bypass procedure for a two-parent notification statute); *Ohio v. Akron Center for Reproductive Health*, 497 U.S. 502, 510 (1990) (requiring bypass procedures for parental consent statutes).

27. *Planned Parenthood of Central Missouri v. Danforth*, 428 U.S. 52, 74 (1976).

28. Fried, Marlene Gerber, *Abortion in the United States: Barriers to Access*, 4 Reproductive and Sexual Rights 174, 182 (2001) (discussing the impact of judicial bypass process on young women); *Hodgson v. Minnesota*, 648 F.Supp. 756, 763–64 (D. Minn. 1986).

29. *Id.*, at 763; Dennis, Amanda, Stanley K. Henshaw, Theodore J. Joyce, Lawrence B. Finer, & Kelly Blanchard. The Guttmacher Institute, *The Impact of Laws Requiring Parental Involvement for Abortion: A Literature Review* at page 3 (March 2009).

30. Helena Silverstein & Leanne Speitel, *"Honey, I Have No Idea": Court Readiness to Handle Petitions to Waive Parental Consent for Abortion*, 88 Iowa L. Rev. 75 (2002); Helena Silverstein, *Girls on the Stand: How Courts Fail Pregnant Minors* (2007).

31. *Hodgson v. Minnesota*, 497 U.S. 417, 420 (1990) (requiring a bypass procedure for a two-parent notification statute); *Ohio v. Akron Center for Reproductive Health*, 497 U.S. 502, 510 (1990) (requiring bypass procedures for parental consent statutes).

32. Excerpt, St. Charles County Juvenile Court, reprinted in *T.L.J. v. Webster*, 792 F.2d 734, 738–739 n.4 (1986).

33. Tamar Lewin, *Parental Consent to Abortion: How Enforcement Can Vary*, N.Y. Times, May 28, 1992, at A1.

34. National Abortion Federation (NAF) and the National Women's Law Center, The Judicial Bypass Procedure Fails to Protect Young Women, (undated) (factsheet).

35. Helena Silverstein, *Road Closed: Evaluating the Judicial Bypass Provision of the Pennsylvania Abortion Control Act*, 24 Law and Social Inquiry 80, 83–84 (1999); NARAL, Deceptive Anti-Abortion Crisis Pregnancy Centers (April 19, 1999), available at http://www.naral.org/mediaresources/fact/pdfs/crisis_pregnancy.pdf (last visited January 21, 2003).

36. *Ex Parte Anonymous*, 812 So.2d 1234 (Alabama, August 16, 2001); Bill Poovey, *Divided Court Upholds Denial of Abortion for Unemotional Teen*, Associated Press, August 17, 2001.

37. Saul D. Hoffman, The National Campaign to Prevent Teen Pregnancy, *By the Numbers: The Public Costs of Teen Childbearing* (October 2006).

38. Namkee Ahn, *Teenage Childbearing and High School Completion: Accounting for Individual Heterogeneity*, 26 Family Planning Perspectives 18 (1994); The National

Campaign to Prevent Teen Pregnancy, *Why It Matters: Teen Pregnancy, Poverty, and Income Disparity* (March 2010) at http://www.thenationalcampaign.org/why-it-matters/pdf/poverty.pdf (last visited October 6, 2010).

39. The National Campaign to Prevent Teen and Unplanned Pregnancy, *Latina Teen Pregnancy and Educational Attainment* (May 2010) at http://www.thenationalcampaign.org/espanol/PDF/latino_education.pdf (last visited October 20, 2010).

40. Saul D. Hoffman, The National Campaign to Prevent Teen Pregnancy, *By the Numbers: The Public Costs of Teen Childbearing* (October 2006).

41. The National Campaign to Prevent Teen Pregnancy, *Why It Matters: Teen Pregnancy, Poverty, and Income Disparity* (March 2010) at http://www.thenationalcampaign.org/why-it-matters/pdf/poverty.pdf (last visited October 6, 2010).

42. The Alan Guttmacher Institute, Sex and America's Teenagers 61–62 (New York: 1994); National Research Council, Risking the Future: Adolescent Sexuality, Pregnancy, and Childbearing 130 (Cheryl D. Hayes ed., National Academy Press 1987); The National Campaign To Prevent Teen Pregnancy, *Why It Matters: Teen Pregnancy, Poverty, and Income Disparity* (March 2010) at http://www.thenationalcampaign.org/why-it-matters/pdf/poverty.pdf (last visited October 6, 2010).

43. Annie E. Casey Foundation, supra note 42; Saul D. Hoffman, The National Campaign to Prevent Teen Pregnancy, *By the Numbers: The Public Costs of Teen Childbearing* (October 2006).

44. The National Campaign to Prevent Teen Pregnancy, *Teen Pregnancy and Overall Child Well-Being*, at http://www.thenationalcampaign.org/why-it-matters/pdf/child_well-being.pdf (last visited October 15, 2010).

45. The National Campaign to Prevent Teen Pregnancy, *Why It Matters: Teen Pregnancy, Poverty, and Income Disparity* (March 2010) at http://www.thenationalcampaign.org/why-it-matters/pdf/poverty.pdf (last visited October 6, 2010).

46. Douglas Kirby, No Easy Answers: Research Findings on Programs to Reduce Teen Pregnancy 47 (The National Campaign to Prevent Teen Pregnancy 1997), available at http://www.teenpregnancy.org/resources/data/report_summaries/no_easy_answers/default.asp. Another review of 23 individual studies found that specific sexuality and AIDS/STD education programs that discuss both abstinence and contraception may have a number of positive effects on adolescents, including postponing initiation of intercourse, reducing the frequency of intercourse and increasing the use of contraceptives. Douglas Kirby et al., *School-Based Programs to Reduce Sexual Risk Behaviors: A Review of Effectiveness*, 109 Public Health Reports 339, 352–353 (1994); Christopher Trenholm et al., Mathematica Policy Research, Inc. *Impacts of four Title V, Section 510 abstinence education programs: Final Report* (April 2007), available at http://www.mathematicampr.com/publications/pdfs/impactabstinence.pdf.

"When a state enacts a parental involvement law, the abortion rate falls by an average of approximately 13.6 percent."

Parental Involvement Laws Reduce Minors' Abortion Rate

Michael New

In the following viewpoint, a political scholar argues that empirical research shows that when states enact parental involvement laws, the abortion rate of minors falls. The author maintains that the stronger the law, the bigger the drop, claiming that parental consent laws reduce abortion rates more than parental notification laws. Additionally, he contends that parental involvement laws that require involvement of two parents, rather than one, reduce the abortion rate to a greater degree. Michael New is an assistant professor of political science at the University of Michigan-Dearborn, a fellow at the Witherspoon Institute in Princeton, New Jersey, and an adjunct scholar at the Charlotte Lozier Institute in Washington, DC.

A 2008 study done by Michael J. New, Ph.D. was the first of its kind to compare different types of parental involvement laws and their effect on reducing the incidence of abortion among minors. This comprehensive analysis of data regarding abortions performed on minors (age 15, 16 and 17-years-old) from nearly all 50 states between 1985 and 1999 demonstrates that state-level parental involvement laws are effective in reducing the incidence of abortion among minors by approximately 14 percent.

The Impact of Parental Involvement Laws on Abortion

While a number of different types of laws result in reductions in minor abortion rates, including informed consent laws, overall, the findings indicate that when a state enacts a parental involvement law, the abortion rate falls by an average of approximately 13.6 percent. The more protective a parental involvement law, the larger the decline in abortion.

Laws that require parental consent instead of parental notification reduce the minor abortion rate by about 19 percent. Furthermore, laws that mandate the involvement of two parents, instead of just one parent, reduce the in-state minor abortion rate by approximately 31 percent. When the age groups are analyzed, the results indicate that the passage of parental involvement laws reduces the abortion rate among 17-year-olds by 18.3 percent, among 16-year-olds by 14.3 percent, and among 15-year-olds, by 8.6 percent. These findings are all considered to be statistically significant. Parental involvement laws do not result in declines in the abortion rate for 18 and 19-year-olds, which is not surprising. These women would be demographically similar to their minor counterparts, but since they are no longer minors, they would not be directly affected by the passage of the parental involvement legislation. This finding provides additional evidence that the abortion decline among minors is caused by the enactment of parental involvement legislation, as opposed to broader cultural factors.

A mother holds her pregnant thirteen-year-old daughter. Studies show that parental involvement laws, especially laws that require the consent of both parents, significantly reduce the rate of abortion by minors. © AP Images/Knoxville News Sentinel, Michael Patrick

The Effects of Parental Involvement Laws

Parental consent laws result in an 18.7 percent decline in minor abortion rates, whereas parental notification laws only result in a decline of around 5 percent. Parental consent laws result in larger abortion declines across all age groups. In each case, these differences achieve conventional standards of statistical significance, providing solid evidence that consent laws are more effective than notification laws.

Parental involvement laws, which require the involvement of two parents, result in larger abortion reductions than laws that require the involvement of only one parent. Overall, laws requiring the involvement of two parents result in a 31.4 percent decline in the minor abortion rate, whereas parental involvement laws requiring the involvement of only one parent result in a minor abortion rate decline of 13.5 percent. This difference

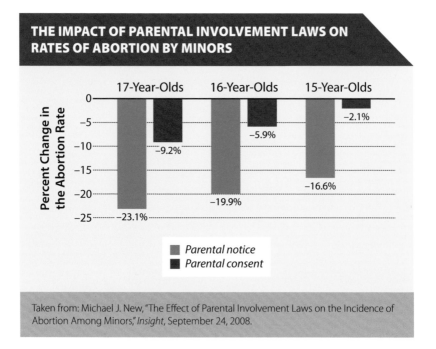

THE IMPACT OF PARENTAL INVOLVEMENT LAWS ON RATES OF ABORTION BY MINORS

Taken from: Michael J. New, "The Effect of Parental Involvement Laws on the Incidence of Abortion Among Minors," *Insight*, September 24, 2008.

is statistically significant. Furthermore, among every age group, legislation requiring the involvement of two parents results in larger abortion declines than laws requiring the involvement of only one parent. Overall, laws that require the involvement of two parents show the most promise for being able to reduce the incidence of abortion among minors.

The overall minor abortion rate in the United States has fallen by close to fifty percent between 1985 and 1999, and New's study shows that parental involvement laws are an important causal factor in this decline. His study provides solid evidence that laws that require parental consent result in larger abortion declines than laws that only require parental notification, and legislation requiring the involvement of two parents results in larger abortion declines than laws requiring the involvement of only one parent. These findings should inform future debates in state legislators about how to best protect unborn children. Currently, about 36 states have a parental involvement law on the books, but some are more effective than others in their ability to reduce the incidence of abortion. The laws that were enacted in Minnesota (requiring two-parent notification) and Mississippi (requiring two-parent consent) were shown to be among the most effective in reducing abortion rates among minors.

> *"These findings suggest that most parental involvement laws have little impact on minors' abortion rate and, by extension, on birthrates and pregnancy rates."*

The Impact of Laws Requiring Parental Involvement for Abortion: A Literature Review

Amanda Dennis, Stanley K. Henshaw, Theodore J. Joyce, Lawrence B. Finer, and Kelly Blanchard

In the following viewpoint, a group of researchers argues that empirical studies have not shown a link between states' enactment of parental involvement laws and a drop in the abortion rate of young women. The authors contend that research does show that the laws cause some minors to travel to other states for abortion or to delay getting an abortion. Amanda Dennis is a senior project manager at Ibis Reproductive Health, where Kelly Blanchard is president. Stanley K. Henshaw is a senior fellow and Lawrence B. Finer is the director of domestic research at the Guttmacher Institute. Theodore J. Joyce is a professor of economics at Baruch College and a research associate with the National Bureau of Economic Research.

A. Dennis et al., excerpted from *The Impact of Laws Requiring Parental Involvement for Abortion: A Literature Review.* New York: Guttmacher Institute, 2009.

Highlights

- In 2008, 34 states had laws in effect that mandated parental involvement in minors' abortions.

- A literature search identified 29 studies of the impact of these laws on a range of outcomes.

- The clearest documented impact of parental involvement laws is an increase in the number of minors traveling outside their home states to obtain abortion services in states that do not mandate parental involvement or that have less restrictive laws.

- Many studies reported a decline in minors' abortion rate associated with parental involvement laws. However, most of these studies did not measure abortions among minors who leave the state, or stop coming into the state, because of the law. Studies in Mississippi and Massachusetts, which incorporated data on minors traveling out of state, found no effect on the abortion rate, while one in Texas suggested that parental involvement laws lower abortion rates and raise birthrates if minors must travel long distances to access providers in states without such laws.

- Several state studies found no short-term impact on pregnancy rates.

- Many studies had serious limitations, including incomplete data, inadequate controls for factors other than the imposition of the law and lack of statistical power because they measured outcomes among all women or teenagers rather than minors. Several reported anomalous findings that indicate confounding by uncontrolled variables.

- Three studies reported large impacts of parental involvement laws on infant and child health. These findings are implausible, given the small or undocumented increase in unintended childbearing and the limited data on infant and child well-being.

• Future research should incorporate straightforward designs with minor-specific data. Researchers should document prelaw trends in outcomes among those exposed and unexposed to the laws. They also should clearly discuss expected outcomes, statistical power and the plausibility of their findings.

Discussion

As this review shows, researchers have used a wide range of strategies to assess the impact of parental involvement laws on multiple outcomes. The clearest impact documented is the increase in the number of minors who travel outside their home states to obtain services in states that do not have such laws or that have less restrictive ones. Studies documented such travel in Massachusetts,[27] Mississippi[28, 39] and Missouri.[36, 37] For example, in Massachusetts, 29% of minors who had abortions did so in neighboring states, most in response to a parental consent requirement.[27] In South Carolina, on the other hand, where the law applied only to minors younger than age 17 and a grandparent could satisfy the consent requirement, no out-of-state travel was detected.[29] A study in Minnesota assumed (without confirmatory data) that no minors went out of state.[40] In Texas, however, relatively few minors evidently did so.[41] In general, the impact of these laws on minors' travel appears to vary widely, depending on the specifics of the requirements, the abortion regulations of surrounding states and the state's geography.

Several studies addressed the core question of the effect of parental involvement laws on minors' rates of abortion, birth and pregnancy. These laws might reduce abortion rates by causing minors either to continue unwanted pregnancies or to take steps to avoid pregnancy. Many of these studies had to make serious compromises in their methodologies, and their results varied widely. The studies that pooled data from all or most states faced obstacles that weakened their results. Most serious was their inability to adequately account for minors who cross state lines to avoid their home state's parental involvement requirement. Such travel would decrease the apparent abortion rate in the restrictive state and increase it in less restrictive and nonrestrictive states even if the total number of abortions was unaffected by the law. In addition, parental involvement laws may reduce the number of minors from other states who would normally have abortions in the state for reasons of convenience or cost. These effects could explain why several studies found that such laws result in a decrease in minors' abortion rates,[26, 32, 38] while few found effects on birthrates.[14, 30]

A number of studies found that the laws were associated with reductions in the abortion rates of women aged 18–19 and older women,[31, 32, 38] or that laws that were not enforced affected abortion rates.[22, 26] Such implausible findings reduce the credibility of the studies and methods, and suggest that uncontrolled factors could account for some or all of the relationships found. Time-series studies that found decreased abortion rates showed a smaller effect when state-specific trends in the abortion rate were accounted for.[14, 21] This finding suggests that in states that enacted parental involvement laws, abortion rates were changing in a different way than they were elsewhere, independently of the effect of the laws.

Several studies found a greater impact on white than on black teenagers,[34, 41] a plausible result, since white minors are more likely than their black counterparts to conceal a pregnancy from their parents. On the other hand, white teenagers are also more likely to have the resources to travel out of state for abortion services.

The state case studies yielded mixed results concerning effects of parental involvement laws on minors' abortion rates. In Massachusetts, the number of abortions was about what would have been expected if preexisting trends had continued and out-of-state abortions were counted.[27] Similarly, the Mississippi law appeared to have little effect on the number of abortions or births.[28, 39] In South Carolina, however, the abortion ratio among white 16-year-olds fell even in analyses that took into account out-of-state terminations.[29] In Minnesota, the number of abortions also fell, with no corresponding increase in births, although the number of minors who sought services out of state is unknown.[36, 40] The clearest result is from Texas, where the abortion rate decreased and the birthrate increased among women slightly younger than age 18 in comparison with women slightly older than this age.[41]

Taken together, these findings suggest that most parental involvement laws have little impact on minors' abortion rate and, by extension, on birthrates and pregnancy rates. However, the Texas study illustrates that in some cases, the laws may compel a small proportion of minors to continue unwanted pregnancies.[41] The similar pattern found in Missouri[37] could be real, or it could reflect missing data on residents' out-of-state abortions.

More controversial are the studies that have looked at the impact of parental involvement laws on minors' pregnancy rates. None of them has definitively shown a reduction in pregnancy rates, and the study of Massachusetts,[27] which had data on abortions performed in other states, found no measurable effect on pregnancies. In Texas, the pregnancy rate of 17-year-olds was unchanged compared with that of 18-year-olds.[42] Since the studies did not find any change in the abortion rates, there is likely no effect on birthrates either. However, one cannot rule out the possibility that over time, minors adjust to parental involvement laws and become more conservative in their sexual behavior. This is difficult to test, however, since the longer a law has been in effect, the greater the confounding is from other factors.

A number of studies analyzed the association between parental involvement laws and the timing of abortion, using changes in mean gestation and the proportion and the rate of second-trimester abortions as outcomes. The results were

According to studies, African American teenagers are less likely to conceal pregnancy from their parents or seek out-of-state abortions. © Image Source/Getty Images.

mixed. Rogers et al.[40] reported no increase in the rate of second-trimester abortions in Minnesota, but they did find an increase in the ratio of late to early abortions. Similarly, Ellertson,[36] using the same data, reported an increase in the odds of abortions after eight weeks' gestation. These seemingly conflicting findings are not contradictory, since the rate can remain unchanged even if the proportion rises. Some evidence suggested that mean gestational age rose in Mississippi after enforcement of a consent statute, but the probability of a second-trimester abortion did not.[39] Data limitations and lack of statistical power hamper the analyses of timing. One issue is that minors who obtain court bypass waivers almost by definition experience at least a few days of delay, and those who travel out of state usually experience even greater delays; however, these are a minority of all minors obtaining abortions. Another issue is that minors who leave the state are usually not included in analyses. The Texas study overcame issues of both a small sample size and out-of-state travel.[41] In that study, the law was associated with a rise in the proportion of second-trimester abortions, but this was limited to minors who were just old enough to delay the termination until they turned 18.

The health outcomes of children born to women who may have been affected by parental involvement laws are also unclear, as the three studies included in this review found differing results. In the first study by Bitler and Zavodny,[45] there was no clear correlation between these laws and child abuse or maltreatment. However, in a similar study two years later, the authors found that such laws led to a decrease in child abuse and maltreatment.[46] They attributed this to fewer teenagers having children, inferring that the presence of these laws in a state leads to change in the sexual or contraceptive behaviors of these youth. Sen,[47] by contrast, found that parental involvement laws were associated with an increase in child abuse and maltreatment. Her design was arguably more sophisticated, since it included information about border states in the model, differentiated between parental involvement and parental consent, and stratified the results by race. However, any effect on child abuse is implausible because it would operate through the effect on unwanted births, and parental involvement laws have at best a small effect on such births.

In conclusion, the studies we reviewed provide important information on and insight into the impact of parental involvement laws on minors. Their limitations highlight areas where novel research design and methodology will be needed. Perhaps equally important are certain gaps in the evidence uncovered by the review. We found no studies that evaluated increased costs in obtaining abortion due to delays, travel or bypass proceedings; the impact on minors of being forced to consult their parents; or minors' opinions about the parental involvement laws. These are also important areas for future study.

Notes

14. Levine PB, Parental involvement laws and fertility behavior, *Journal of Health Economics*, 2003, 22(5):861–878.

. . .

21. Matthews S, Ribar D and Wilhelm M, The effects of economic conditions and access to reproductive health services on state abortion rates and birthrates, *Family Planning Perspectives*, 1997, 29(2):52–60.
22. Bitler M and Zavodny M, The effect of abortion restrictions on the timing of abortions, *Journal of Health Economics*, 2001, 20(6):1011–1032.

. . .

26. Haas-Wilson D, The impact of state abortion restrictions on minors' demand for abortions, *Journal of Human Resources*, 1996, 31(1):140–158.
27. Cartoof VG and Klerman LV, Parental consent for abortion: impact of the Massachusetts law, *American Journal of Public Health*, 1986, 76(4):397–400.
28. Henshaw SK, The impact of requirements for parental consent on minors' abortions in Mississippi, *Family Planning Perspectives*, 1995, 27(3):120–122.
29. Joyce T and Kaestner R, State reproductive policies and adolescent pregnancy resolution: the case of parental involvement laws, *Journal of Health Economics*, 1996, 15(5):579–607.
30. Kane T and Staiger D, Teen motherhood and abortion access, *The Quarterly Journal of Economics*, 1996, 111(2):467–506.
31. Medoff MH, Price restriction and abortion demand, *Journal of Family and Economic Issues*, 2007, 28(4):583–599.
32. New MJ, *Analyzing the Effect of State Legislation on the Incidence of Abortion Among Minors*, Washington, DC: Heritage Foundation, 2007, Center for Data Analysis Report 07–01.

. . .

34. Klick J and Stratmann T, Abortion access and risky sex among teens: parental involvement laws and sexually transmitted diseases, *Journal of Law, Economics, and Organization*, 2008, 24(1):2–21.

. . .

36. Ellertson C, Mandatory parental involvement in minors' abortions: effects of the laws in Minnesota, Missouri, and Indiana, *American Journal of Public Health*, 1997, 87(8):1367–1374.
37. Pierson V, Missouri's parental consent laws and teen pregnancy outcomes, *Women & Health*, 1995, 22(3):47–57.
38. Tomal A, Parental involvement laws and minor and non-minor teen abortion and birth rates, *Journal of Family and Economic Issues*, 1999, 20(2):149–162.
39. Joyce T and Kaestner R, The impact of mandatory waiting periods and parental consent laws on the timing of abortion and state of occurrence among adolescents in Mississippi and South Carolina, *Journal of Policy Analysis and Management*, 2001, 20(2):263–282.
40. Rogers JL et al., Impact of the Minnesota parental notification law on abortion and birth, *American Journal of Public Health*, 1991, 81(3):294–298.
41. Joyce T, Kaestner R and Colman S, Changes in abortions and births and the Texas parental notification law, *New England Journal of Medicine*, 2006, 354(10):1031–1038.
42. Colman S, Joyce T and Kaestner R, Misclassification bias and the estimated effect of parental involvement laws on adolescents' reproductive outcomes, *American Journal of Public Health*, 2008, 98(10):1881–1885.

Abortion

. . .

45. Bitler M and Zavodny M, Child abuse and abortion availability, *American Economic Review*, 2002, 92(2):363–367.
46. Bitler M and Zavodny M, Child maltreatment, abortion availability, and economic conditions, *Review of Economics of the Household*, 2004, 2(2):119–141.
47. Sen B, State abortion restrictions and child fatal injury: an exploratory study, *Southern Economic Journal*, 2007, 73(3):553–574.

▌ *"Reproductive freedom is in trouble."*

Beyond Apocalypse and Apology: A Moral Defense of Abortion

Caitlin Borgmann and Catherine Weiss

In the following viewpoint, two lawyers argue that the movement to support reproductive freedom has grown complacent, even in the face of myriad restrictions that increasingly make it difficult for low-income women and teenagers to exercise their rights under Roe v. Wade. The authors contend that rather than taking an apocalyptic or an apologetic approach to abortion, supporters of reproductive freedom should defend abortion as a moral choice that upholds the autonomy and equality of women. Caitlin Borgmann is a professor of law at the City University of New York School of Law, and Catherine Weiss is senior counsel and director of Public Interest Advocacy for the Lowenstein Center for the Public Interest.

The movement to preserve and advance reproductive freedom is suffering the consequences of a great victory. The

C. Borgmann and C. Weiss, "Beyond Apocalypse and Apology: A Moral Defense of Abortion," *Family Planning Perspectives*, 2003, vol. 35, no. 1, pp. 40–43.

establishment of the constitutional right to abortion in *Roe v. Wade* was a monumental step that changed the lives of American women. Girls grow up today under the mantle of *Roe*, never having known a world in which illegal, unsafe, degrading and sometimes fatal abortions were the norm. That is a cause for celebration as *Roe* turns 30. It is also, however, a cause of complacency. Movements typically subside after winning major legal or political battles, and ours has not escaped this cycle.

Complacency corrodes all freedoms. It is particularly dangerous to reproductive freedom because our opponents are single-minded and fervent to the point of fanaticism. Their crusade has fueled three decades of incremental restrictions that make it risky or burdensome to get an abortion and, for some women, block access altogether. Understandably, the prochoice movement has grown frustrated with the unending onslaught, and the public, numb. The movement's responses to this conundrum have varied over time and among its many spokespersons. Yet, two recurring approaches—to jolt the public by forecasting *Roe*'s reversal and to court reluctant supporters by steering wide of abortion altogether—are problematic. We need to recapture at least some of the moral urgency that led to *Roe*, and we must meet the assaults head-on.

Reproductive freedom is in trouble. The Supreme Court has refrained from overturning *Roe* but has allowed the states to layer myriad restrictions on abortion. The states, seizing the opportunity to regulate women's lives, enacted more than 300 restrictions on access to abortion and other reproductive health services between 1995 and 2001.[1] Some of the most common laws affect all women seeking abortions in a particular state: For example, 18 states require counseling designed to dissuade women from having abortions, followed by a waiting period before an abortion can be performed.[2]

The assault on *Roe* has done the most damage, however, to women whose voices are largely ignored in the political debate and whose interests carry the least political weight. Low-income women face what can be prohibitive costs in seeking abortions. Very few have private health insurance, and government-supported plans rarely pay for abortions. Moreover, these women face significant financial obstacles merely to get to a provider. Nationwide, 87% of all counties lack abortion providers (because of inadequate training opportunities for medical students, burdensome regulations targeted at abortion providers, and a climate of harassment and violence, among other factors).[3] For low-income women living in rural areas, this can mean adding costs for travel, time away from jobs and child care to the cost of the abortion itself.

Teenagers have also suffered the brunt of abortion restrictions. More than half the states enforce laws that deny those younger than 18 access to a legal abortion unless they involve a parent or go to court.[4] Teenagers who consult their parents under compulsion of the law and against their better judgment often find their fears justified: They are kicked out of their homes, beaten and prevented from obtaining abortions. The alternative of going to court is daunting for any teenager, and especially for one who is pregnant, desperate and unsupported by her family. Often, she must explain multiple absences from school without raising suspicions, find a lawyer who will help her, brave one or more trips to the courthouse, tell the intimate details of her personal life to numerous strangers and then hope that the judge grants her the permission she needs.

Yet, advocates for reproductive freedom tire of talking about these restrictions, and few people seem interested in hearing about them. Because most middle-class, adult women can get abortions in spite of the prevalent restrictions, the majoritarian passion to preserve the right established in *Roe* has faded, leaving the most vulnerable women isolated and powerless. They have reason to wonder what we are celebrating at *Roe*'s anniversary.

What we need to celebrate is renewed unity, commitment, energy and purpose. Unfortunately, the movement has sometimes tried to achieve these by either dwelling on the possibility

Pro-choice activists demonstrate in favor of women's reproductive rights. In the United States, 87 percent of all counties lack abortion providers. © Laima Druskis/Photo Researchers/Getty Images.

that abortion will again be illegal or minimizing the importance of abortion. We refer to these two tendencies as the apocalyptic and the apologetic approaches.

The Apocalyptic Approach

The apocalyptic approach aims to rouse the public from complacency by positing an immediate and personal threat: Women will no longer be able to get an abortion when they need one. This approach recognizes that a woman who thinks that the abortion rights battle is over and won can be goaded into action if she is convinced that the victory is about to be reversed and that its reversal will affect her. The threat posed must be imminent, real and personal.

Typically, the apocalyptic approach warns that the Supreme Court is on the brink of overturning *Roe v. Wade*. To emphasize the immediacy of the threat, this approach highlights the hostility of the current administration and the advancing age of several justices who support women's right to choose. Focusing on the worst-case scenario—the Court's complete overturning of *Roe*—makes the threat personal to a broad swath of Americans. Thus, this approach hopes to draw in people who are not moved to activism in opposition to narrower restrictions.

There can be no doubt that the already battered right declared in *Roe* faces new and powerful assaults. Both the White House and the Congress are enemies of choice and stand prepared to appoint and confirm like-minded judges—not only to the Supreme Court, but also to the lower federal courts where most abortion rights cases are decided. In addition, Congress is now in a position to pass long-threatened federal restrictions, posing yet more obstacles to abortion nationwide.

The question remains, however, whether these assaults will prove fatal to *Roe* itself. If history is any guide, the Supreme Court may well continue to say that *Roe* is good law while upholding one restriction after another. This is the compromise the Court adopted in the late 1980s and openly embraced in its 1992 decision in *Planned Parenthood v. Casey*. The Court there proclaimed, "the essential holding of *Roe v. Wade* should be retained and once again reaffirmed," but then added, "the fact that a law . . . has the incidental effect of making it more difficult or more expensive to procure an abortion cannot be enough to invalidate it."[5] If the Court follows this pattern, the damage, while devastating, will continue to be incremental, cumulative and obscure, rather than dramatic, sudden and obvious. Of course, the harms will accumulate faster as the courts grow more hostile.

Because a candid reversal of Roe is neither certain nor immediate, people may react to constant warnings as they would to a car alarm that goes off at all hours—it is annoying, but they learn to ignore it. We risk being unable to galvanize the public if and when we confront the imminent possibility of *Roe*'s demise.

Moreover, constantly referring to the possibility of losing the "core right" to abortion diverts attention from the significant encroachments that have already been and continue to be placed on the right. Under this approach, whether the core right exists is effectively measured by whether a middle-class, adult woman has access to an abortion. Meanwhile, a low-income woman has, for all intents and purposes, already lost her core right if she depends on Medicaid for her medical care but is denied coverage for an abortion; if she lives in a rural state with no abortion provider within 200 miles; and if she must make two trips to that distant provider, thanks to a state-imposed waiting period. Her right is a hollow promise when the government is permitted to erect so many hurdles that they create an impasse.

The Apologetic Approach

The apologetic approach takes a different tack. Reacting to a widespread and apparently growing discomfort with abortion, it focuses predominantly on topics the public finds more palatable, such as contraception and sexuality education. It minimizes discussion of abortion, or characterizes abortion as regrettably necessary.

This approach hopes to garner additional supporters for the movement's overall agenda by beginning with more popular subjects. Unfortunately, it does not always proceed from there. Bringing people into the fold by first discussing different (though related) issues may create an opening to convince them about the importance of access to abortion, but it is not a substitute.

The apologetic approach also hopes to draw people in by identifying with their misgivings about abortion. Respect for uncertainties and objections is critical to any conversation about deeply held values, but the apologetic approach does not engage in moral dialogue. Instead, it mirrors the public's general skittishness about abortion.

The tendency to shy from open discussion of and support for abortion plays into the hands of our opponents. They want the public to associate abortion with secrecy, trauma, stigma, guilt, fear and shame. Both our silence and our apologies reinforce these associations, however unintentionally. Our opponents say that abortion is murder, we imply or say that it is regrettable, and the public slides further into ambivalence. Recent polling data suggest such slippage in public support.[6]

Furthermore, the apologetic approach tacitly promotes the myth that the prochoice movement is too extreme. This approach calls for putting on a fresh and friendly face, to contrast with the glare of the stereotypical radical feminist. But we have not been frowning on childbearing, fighting for abortion on demand until moments before birth or generally scorning the views of the public. We do not need to pursue moderation as though we have been guilty of extremism.

When we smile brightly and sidestep the issue of abortion, we risk alienating our strongest supporters. They understand that abortion rights are part of a larger constellation of both rights and aspirations. We stand not only for the right to choose, but also for comprehensive sexuality education, effective contraceptive options, quality prenatal care and childbirth assistance, and trustworthy and affordable child care. Focusing on abortion to the exclusion of all else is a mistake—but so is avoiding the subject of abortion. When we are evasive, our supporters may doubt our commitment, even if they understand that our evasiveness reflects a tactical strategy rather than a shift in principle. They may wonder about the effectiveness of outreach efforts that omit or equivocate about so important a topic and, thus, forgo the opportunity to educate people about the ongoing, cumulative damage to abortion rights.

In its hesitance to defend abortion, the apologetic approach shrinks from the wrong demon. It is an unwanted or unhealthy pregnancy that causes a woman to confront the abortion decision. Once she is in this predicament, abortion may be a welcome solution among very limited options. Bemoaning abortion is like lamenting open-heart surgery in the face of Americans' unacceptably high rate of heart disease. We hope never to need a coronary bypass, but we are grateful to have the procedure available if we need it.

Similarly, as critics of the apologetic approach have pointed out, "One can feel bad, sorry, or regretful that any woman ever has an unwanted pregnancy. One can also feel truly wonderful that safe abortions are legally available when wanted."[7] These are not contradictory positions.

Abortion as a Moral Choice

An alternative to the apocalyptic and apologetic approaches is a realistic, direct defense that recalls the reasons we fought for legal abortion in the first place. It argues forcefully to a generation that expects equality that without the right to decide whether to continue a pregnancy, a woman's autonomy and equality are compromised. It documents the critical role that access to abortion has played in women's lives over the past 30 years. Rather than focusing on whether we are about to lose *Roe* altogether, it exposes, defends against and attempts to reverse the constant whittling away that diminishes the right to abortion every year. It focuses attention on the unfairness of laws that in effect deny this right to the most vulnerable women.

To defend abortion with confidence, we must first recognize that institutional opposition to the right is part of a broader campaign to undermine women's autonomy and equality. Antichoice leaders see sexuality (especially women's) divorced from procreation as shameful, women as inadequate to make weighty moral decisions and forced childbearing as appropriate punishment for sexual irresponsibility. They approve of requiring women to pay out of pocket for contraception, while ensuring that insurance plans cover men's access to Viagra; reducing sexuality education to a "just say no" mantra and consigning those teenagers who say yes to the deadly risks of unprotected sex; and denying poor women the means to obtain abortions, yet refusing to help them provide adequate food, shelter and education for the children they bear. Abortion is only one piece of the puzzle.

When this puzzle is assembled, the image that emerges is of a woman subjugated, not a fetus saved. For example, it is illumi-

Barriers to Abortion

Too many women in the United States today face unnecessary barriers when seeking abortion care. Throughout the U.S., there can be a shortage of providers willing to provide abortions and a declining number of hospitals that provide abortion services, which can make it extremely difficult for women to obtain care, especially in rural areas.

National Abortion Federation, "About Access."
www.prochoice.org.

nating that "right-to-life" leaders generally tolerate abortion in cases of rape or incest. The fetus conceived by rape is biologically and morally indistinguishable from the fetus conceived by voluntary intercourse. But in the view of our opponents, the rape victim is innocent while the woman who chooses to have sex is tainted. For them, it is the woman's innocence or guilt that determines whether she should be allowed to have an abortion or forced to bear a child.

The impulse to punish women rather than to help children is equally evident in the policies of antichoice states with regard to children already born. If the motivation behind abortion restrictions were really the love of babies, antichoice states should have child-friendly laws. Yet the opposite is so. A comprehensive review of the abortion and child welfare policies in the 50 states demonstrates that the states with the most restrictive abortion laws also spend the least to facilitate adoption, to provide subsistence to poor children and to educate children in general.[8] The study concludes, "Pro-life states are less likely than pro-choice states to provide adequate care to poor and needy children. Their concern for the weak and vulnerable appears to stop at birth." The seemingly contradictory coexistence of "prolife" laws and antichild policies is explained, in significant part, by opposition to women's changing roles in society: The more hostile statewide public opinion is toward women's equality and the lower women's income is relative to men's, the more likely the state is both to restrict abortion and to impoverish children.[9]

In contrast, our position is prowoman, profamily, prochild and prochoice. This is a moral debate we must have and can win. Such a debate can move doubters to become moral defenders of a woman's decision to have an abortion. Even those who remain personally opposed to abortion may come to support each woman's right to make the decision in accordance with her own conscience, commitments and beliefs. What follows are some of the best reasons to support abortion rights.

Autonomy

A woman deciding whether to continue a pregnancy stands on moral ground. She is entitled to make her decision, and she must live with the consequences. No one else—and certainly not the government—should decide whether she will use her body to bring new life into the world. The decision is too intimate and too important to be taken from her.

In everyday life, men and women make decisions that affect the life and death of existing people. They decide whether to join the army; whether to donate blood, a kidney or bone marrow to a child; whether to give money to Save the Children instead of buying a new sweater, whether to decline a lifesaving blood transfusion; whether to drive a small fort on wheels that may protect its passengers in a crash but often kills those in less-substantial vehicles. Few question adults' autonomy to make these decisions, although some may criticize the individual choice made.

Yet, our opponents want a different standard to govern women's decisions about abortion. They portray women who demand the right to make this decision as selfish and immoral, although even many "prolifers" place fetuses on a lower moral plane than existing people (hence their tolerance of abortion in cases of rape and incest, among other inconsistencies). In response, we must staunchly defend women's ability and right to be moral actors, especially when they are making decisions about reproduction.

Equality

Without the right of reproductive choice, women cannot participate equally in the nation's social, political and economic life. Their freedom to decide whether and when to have children opens doors that would otherwise be closed. They may learn to be electricians, librarians, roofers, teachers or triathletes; care for their young children or aging parents; start and finish college; wait until they are financially and emotionally prepared to support a child; keep a steady job; marry if and when they want to.

Women still do the bulk of the work of raising children and caring for extended families. Whether they experience this work as a privilege, a necessity, a burden or all three, increasing their control over the scope and timing of these responsibilities can only help them to secure a more equal footing on whatever paths they travel. In fact, in countries throughout the world, women's desire and ability to limit the number of children they have go hand in hand with their educational advancement and economic independence.

Bodily Integrity

Women should have control over their own bodies. In virtually all other contexts, the law treats a person's body as inviolable. Prisoners are denied many of their most important personal liberties, yet are protected from unreasonable invasions of their bodies (such as routine body cavity searches). Similarly, the state cannot require a crime victim to undergo an operation to recover evidence (such as a bullet), even if that evidence would help to convict a murder suspect. And no law can force an unwilling parent to undergo bodily invasions far less risky than pregnancy (such as donating bone marrow) to save a living child. "It is difficult to imagine a clearer case of bodily intrusion" than for the government to demand that a woman continue a pregnancy and go through childbirth against her will.[10]

Wantedness and Welcome

The decision to have a child—even more than the decision to have an abortion—carries profound moral implications. Unless a woman is willing to bear a child and give it up for adoption, she should have children when she feels she can welcome them. A mother's freedom to decide whether and when to have an additional child contributes immeasurably to the welfare of the children she already has, as well as any yet to be born. A teenager's decision to delay having a child until a time when she can provide adequate financial and emotional support increases the probability that when she does decide to have a family, it will be healthy and stable. Indeed, many women who decide not to have a child at a particular time do so out of reverence for children.

Personal and Public Health

Finally, the right to abortion promotes personal and public health. We know that criminal bans do not stop women from seeking abortions. The desperate measures women in pre-*Roe* days felt driven to take to terminate their unwanted pregnancies are testament to how untenable the prospect of childbearing can be. Access to safe, legal abortion ensures that women will not be maimed or killed when they decide they cannot continue a pregnancy. Similarly, access to safe abortion ensures that women can terminate pregnancies that endanger their health. A pregnant woman with a heart condition, uncontrolled hypertension, diabetes or one of a host of other problems must have all medically accepted options open to her. She, her loved ones and her doctor must be able to respond to shifting and serious health risks without having to consult a lawyer.

Conclusion

These reasons to support abortion rights are not new. All of them predate *Roe v. Wade*, some by centuries. Yet, as *Roe* turns 30 and continues its embattled advance toward middle age, these reasons are as pressing as ever. We state them in different ways to appeal to different audiences at different times, but all provide a basis for persuading people to stand behind abortion rights, both for themselves and for others.

However persuasive we are, of course, a groundswell to defend the right to abortion may not rise up until enough people feel so personally threatened that they take action. Nevertheless, if we are clear, straightforward and unabashed about why we advocate for reproductive freedom, and realistic about the threats we face, we may rebuild public support, even if this support does not instantly translate into activism. Maintaining and reinforcing this support can, in turn, ready the public for a call to action. Thus, we preserve the best hope not only for mobilizing in a crisis, but also for targeted organizing against the disparate restrictions that are building into a barrier too high for many to cross.

References

1. National Abortion and Reproductive Rights Action League (NARAL), *Who Decides? A State-by-State Review of Abortion and Reproductive Rights*, Washington, DC: NARAL, 2002, p. 1.
2. NARAL, "Informed" consent/waiting periods, <http://www.naral.org/media resources/publications/2002/sub_informed.pdf>, accessed Dec. 3, 2002.
3. Finer LB and Henshaw SK, Abortion incidence and services in the United States in 2000, *Perspectives on Sexual and Reproductive Health*, 2003, 35(1):6–15.
4. NARAL, Minors' access, <http://www.naral.org/mediaresources/publications/2002/ sub_minors_access.pdf>, accessed Dec. 3, 2002.
5. *Planned Parenthood v. Casey*, 505 U.S. 833, 846, 874 (1992).
6. Lake Snell Perry & Associates and American Viewpoint, Findings based on a survey of 1,375 registered voters and four focus groups, paper presented at the annual meeting of the Planned Parenthood Federation of America, Washington, DC, Mar. 21–23, 2002, p. 88; and Saad L, Public opinion about abortion—an in-depth review, <http:// www. gallup.com/poll/specialReports/pollSummaries/sr020122iii.asp?Version=p>, accessed Dec. 3, 2002.
7. Alstad D and Kramer J, Abortion and the morality wars: taking the moral offensive, <http://www.rit.org/editorials/abortion/moralwar.html>, accessed Dec. 3, 2002.

8. Schroedel JR, *Is the Fetus a Person? A Comparison of Policies Across the Fifty States*, Ithaca, NY: Cornell University Press, 2000, pp. 153–157.
9. Ibid., pp. 159–162 & 164.
10. Tribe LH, *American Constitutional Law*, Mineola, NY: Foundation Press, 1988, p. 1340.

> *"The prevailing view used to be: Abortion may be evil, but it's necessary. Increasingly, the sentiment is: Abortion may be necessary, but it's evil."*

There Is a Growing Aversion to Abortion, Especially Among Teens

Steve Chapman

In the following viewpoint, a columnist argues that although the US Supreme Court's decision in Roe v. Wade *made abortion legal, sentiments about abortion have grown more negative over the years, particularly among young people. The author claims that part of the explanation for the growing aversion to abortion is better information about fetal development. He contends that this change in attitudes has resulted in a transformation of behavior, with the abortion rate declining in recent years. Steve Chapman is an editorial writer for the* Chicago Tribune.

The abortion debate has raged since 1973, when the Supreme Court gave abortion constitutional protection, but the basic law of the land has proved immutable. Abortion is legal, and it's going to remain legal for a long time.

A Change in Attitudes

Laws often alter attitudes, inducing people to accept things—such as racial integration—they once rejected. But sometimes, attitudes move in the opposite direction, as people see the consequences of the change. That's the case with abortion.

The news that the abortion rate has fallen to its lowest level in 30 years elicits various explanations, from increased use of contraceptives to lack of access to abortion clinics. But maybe the chief reason is that the great majority of Americans, even many who see themselves as pro-choice, are deeply uncomfortable with it.

In 1992, a Gallup/*Newsweek* poll found 34 percent of Americans thought abortion "should be legal under any circumstances," with 13 percent saying it should always be illegal. Last year [2007], only 26 percent said it should always be allowed, with 18 percent saying it should never be permitted.

Sentiments are even more negative among the group that might place the highest value on being able to escape an unwanted pregnancy: young people. In 2003, Gallup found, one of every three kids from age 13 to 17 said abortion should be illegal in all circumstances. More revealing yet is that 72 percent said abortion is "morally wrong."

By now, pro-life groups know that outlawing most abortions is not a plausible aspiration. So they have adopted a two-pronged strategy. The first is to regulate it more closely—with parental notification laws, informed consent requirements and a ban on partial-birth abortion. The second is to educate Americans with an eye toward changing "hearts and minds." In both, they have had considerable success.

A Transformation in Behavior

Even those who insist Americans are solidly in favor of legal abortion implicitly acknowledge the widespread distaste. That's why the Democratic Party's 2004 platform omitted any mention of the issue, and why politicians who support abortion rights cloak them in euphemisms like "the right to choose."

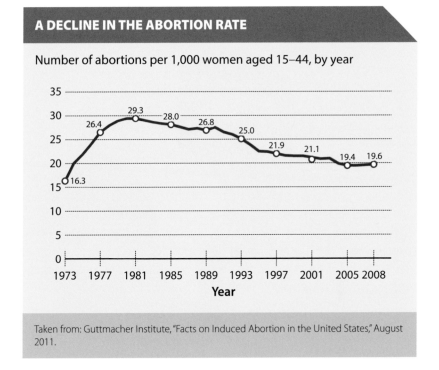

A DECLINE IN THE ABORTION RATE

Number of abortions per 1,000 women aged 15–44, by year

Taken from: Guttmacher Institute, "Facts on Induced Abortion in the United States," August 2011.

But some abortion rights supporters admit reservations. It was a landmark moment in 1995 when the pro-choice author Naomi Wolf, writing in *The New Republic* magazine, declared that "the death of a fetus is a real death." She went on: "By refusing to look at abortion within a moral framework, we lose the millions of Americans who want to support abortion as a legal right but still need to condemn it as a moral iniquity."

The report on abortion rates from the Guttmacher Institute suggests that the evolution of attitudes has transformed behavior. Since 1990, the number of abortions has dropped from 1.61 million to 1.21 million. The abortion rate among women of childbearing age has declined by 29 percent.

Those changes could be the result of other factors, such as more use of contraception: If fewer women get pregnant, fewer will resort to abortion. But the shift is equally marked among

Actress Ellen Page and actor Michael Cera are the stars of the film Juno, *in which Page plays a pregnant teen who decides not to have an abortion.* © Matt Carr/Getty Images Entertainment/ Getty Images.

women who do get pregnant. In 1990, 30.4 percent of pregnancies ended in abortion. Last year, the figure was 22.4 percent.

Pro-choice groups say women are having fewer abortions only because abortion clinics are growing scarcer. But abortion clinics may be growing scarcer because of a decline in demand for their services and a public opinion climate that has gotten more inhospitable.

An Increase in Information

This growing aversion to abortion may be traced to better information. When the Supreme Court legalized abortion in 1973, most people had little understanding of fetal development. But the proliferation of ultrasound images from the womb, combined with the dissemination of facts by pro-life groups, has lifted the veil.

In the new [2007] comedy [film] *Juno*, a pregnant 16-year-old heads for an abortion clinic, only to change her mind after a teenage protester tells her, "Your baby probably has a beating heart, you know. It can feel pain. And it has fingernails."

Juno has been faulted as a "fairy tale" that sugarcoats the realities of teen pregnancy. But if it's a fairy tale, that tells something about how abortion violates our most heartfelt ideals—and those of our adolescent children. Try to imagine a fairy tale in which the heroine has an abortion and lives happily ever after.

The prevailing view used to be: Abortion may be evil, but it's necessary. Increasingly, the sentiment is: Abortion may be necessary, but it's evil.

| "We really need the help of voters and of younger people to save their ability to make their own choices."

The Attorney Who Successfully Argued *Roe v. Wade* Recounts Her Experience

Personal Narrative

Sarah Weddington, interviewed by Martha Burk

In the following viewpoint, a radio host profiles the attorney who argued the US Supreme Court case Roe v. Wade *in support of a woman's right to choose abortion. The attorney explains her experience coming before the court and her concerns that the court is not as supportive of women's reproductive rights as it was in 1973. She claims that the attacks on the right to abortion are now focused on making abortion unavailable rather than illegal and contends that young people need to be aware of the value of the rights that women have gained. Sarah Weddington is an attorney and founder of the Weddington Center. Martha Burk is director of* the Corporate Accountability Project for the National Council of Women's Organizations and host of the public radio show Equal Time with Martha Burk.

January 22 [2012] marks the 39th anniversary of *Roe v. Wade*, the landmark Supreme Court decision that legalized abortion in the United States. That decision has been called the most significant of the 20th century. Certainly it was the most significant for women.

The Experience of an Abortion Advocate

The case was argued by a 27-year-old female lawyer from Texas—Sarah Weddington, in her first appearance before the Court. Female lawyers were so rare in those days that the Supreme Court lawyers' lounge didn't even have a ladies room. There were no female judges. Weddington faced a wall of older white men.

Almost forty years later, Sarah Weddington is still a tireless advocate for women. She now teaches leadership at the University of Texas, writes and speaks nationwide, and continues to educate young women and men on rights and responsibilities, and the fragile nature of progress without vigilance. I took a look back (and a look forward) with her last week [in January 2012] on my radio show, *Equal Time with Martha Burk*. Some highlights:

[Martha Burk:] When you argued the case, you were a young inexperienced lawyer. Were you scared?

[Sarah Weddington:] Well, yes. I cared so much about the result. I was the only person that would be allowed to speak to the Court for the plaintiffs, asking them to overturn the restrictive Texas law. So it was fear-invoking, awe-inspiring, and something you just want so much to win you can taste it.

You won the case 7-2. It seems like every decision that comes out of the Court now is 5-4. Is the Court more politicized now than it was then?

I think it definitely is, particularly on the issue of abortion. Now you have several judges who are very strongly in favor of *Roe v. Wade*, but you also have several who are strongly against. We have two women judges that we're not absolutely sure what their position is going to be. They didn't really talk about it in their confirmation hearings, and the Court hasn't had a case [on *Roe*] since they've been on it.

You did something very unusual when you testified against Clarence Thomas. You brought a picture of a pregnant Thomas to the confirmation hearing.

Yes. He had made some comments that were so outrageous and controversial, and I was trying to say that if he had ever been in the position to be pregnant, he would have much more sympathy and understanding of the way women feel when they're pregnant and don't want to be. There are so many in such dire economic straits—many couples who both have to work to take care of their families, and there is no day care. If Thomas could appreciate the position so many are in, he would understand why it should not be his decision, it should not be the government's decision. They should have a right of privacy on when to continue and when to terminate a pregnancy.

The Rights Underpinning *Roe v. Wade*

Did the case hang primarily on the right to privacy?

Yes. We had in our Supreme Count packets these documents from previous cases where the Supreme Court had said there is a right to privacy in the use of contraception. We were trying to

Sarah Weddington argued the landmark 1973 case of Roe v. Wade *in favor of a woman's right to choose.* © Diana Walker/Time & Life Pictures/Getty Images.

get them to pull that rubber band a little wider, and say it also covers the decision of whether to continue or terminate a pregnancy. But when you argue a case before the Supreme Court you will argue anything that you think might be possible, so we had many [other possible arguments], in other words several parts of the Constitution that might apply.

It seems the opposition is no longer attacking the right to abortion head on—they're concentrating more on onerous restrictions—waiting periods, mandatory sonograms, clinic size requirements and the like.

There is a real split in the opposition. Most of the opposition in recent years has not concentrated on making abortion illegal. They're waiting for the Supreme Court to change so they can win. Instead they want to make it unavailable. [These restrictions] belittle women and their families who try to make the best decision for their own situations.

Given the [Chief Justice John] Roberts Court, do you believe a successful challenge will be argued on the privacy issue or will it be "fetal rights" or even "fertilized egg bills" trying to declare that eggs have the same rights as everyone else?

Even that would probably have several [affirmative] votes on the Court. But the voters have turned down similar laws, most recently in Mississippi [in November 2011]. So the voters have said there are some things you should not have the government deciding. I trust the voters on those cases more than I do the U.S. Supreme Court.

Do you see the fervor in young people today? Or do they think we've got their rights won?

I do see young people trying to help, supporting Planned Parenthood. But I'd say far greater numbers are having such a hard time just going to work, getting money for school and the like. So it's harder for them, but I wish somehow we could get their attention. Part of it is for young people to know what they have now that women didn't have before. We never want to go back to the way it was. And we really need the help of voters and of younger people to save their ability to make their own choices.

You teach leadership at the University of Texas. If you could give only one piece of advice to young people today, what would it be?

Leadership is about leaving your thumb print—a concept of trying to leave the world a better place for others. So I would say to young people, ask yourself, what can I do and how can I leave the world a better place than I found it.

| "It's not your body, it's not your choice,
because you got that from God."

The Plaintiff from *Roe v. Wade* Explains Her Conversion Against Abortion

Personal Narrative

Norma McCorvey, interviewed by Frank Pavone

In the following viewpoint, a pro-life activist interviews the plaintiff who won the right to legal abortion for women in Roe v. Wade. She converted from being pro-choice and working for an abortion doctor to becoming pro-life and against abortion in all circumstances. She contends that other women are also starting to convert from pro-choice to pro-life. Norma McCorvey is the author of Won by Love *and is active in the pro-life movement. Frank Pavone is national director for Priests for Life and Missionaries of the Gospel of Life and president of the National Pro-Life Religious Council.*

Since her conversion to Christianity and to the pro-life cause, Norma McCorvey, the plaintiff in the *Roe vs. Wade* decision,

Norma McCorvey, interviewed by Frank Pavone, "An Interview with Norma McCorvey, the 'Roe' of *Roe v. Wade*." Priests for Life, 1997.

has been a friend of Priests for Life and of Fr. Frank Pavone. This summer (1997) she will appear on the third edition of Fr. Frank's *Defending Life* television series on the Eternal Word Television Network. Her new book, *Won by Love,* telling the marvelous story of her conversion from the abortion industry, will soon be available.

Following is a transcript of an interview held with Norma shortly after her conversion to the Way of Life. An audiotape of this interview is available from Priests for Life.

Frank Pavone: This is Father Frank Pavone and I am here with Norma McCorvey. We're going to talk a little bit about her experiences and her convictions. Norma, thank you very much for being with us.

Norma McCorvey: And thank you for having me, Father.

Norma, we've talked on a good number of occasions, and have shared the joy of what has happened to you, but for the sake of those who are listening to this tape, you are the Jane Roe of Roe vs. Wade.

Yes, Father, I *was* the Jane Roe of *Roe vs. Wade,* but Jane Roe has been laid to rest.

Tell us a little bit about how that happened.

Well, for quite some time Jane Roe/Norma McCorvey had been looking for a spiritual path that she could believe in and feel solid in. And, Operation Rescue moved next to the abortion mill that I worked for, on April 1, a year ago, this past April. And Reverend Benham, started sharing the Gospel of Jesus Christ with me.

And, so in other words his office was next to your abortion facility where you were working. And how did that contact begin? Did they approach you, or how did that happen?

You know, I think it was kind of a mutual thing. I had made kind of a deal with them: I asked them if they did not bring out the place card of Malachi, [a poster of an aborted child], that I would let them have two minutes with each one of my patients.

Malachi is one of those . . .

It's the 21-week-old fetus found in Dallas about four years ago, I believe. So, we honored each other's wishes, and they didn't put out the place cards and I let them have two minutes with each one of my patients.

Going back to the early 70's when the Roe vs. Wade *case was going up through the courts, when you initially got involved in that whole process, did you ever think or did it ever occur to you that it would become such a landmark case?*

Absolutely not Father. I was very politically naïve at the time. I thought that I wanted to have an abortion with the baby that I was carrying, but I had no idea that it would lead up to such a controversial issue.

As I understand from your own autobiography, you did not go looking for these attorneys to try to make abortion legal.

No, sir, quite the contrary. The adoption attorney that was handling the adoption case for my baby told me of these attorneys. They were Sarah Weddington and Linda Coffey. They were trying to overcome the Texas statute on abortion.

And, so they approached you.

Yes, sir. Henry McCloskey, Jr. arranged the first initial meeting. And we met and we discussed, for the first time in my life, reproductive rights.

For the first time in your life it was a discussion.

Yes, sir.

Norma, at that point, and later as your case progressed and after it was decided, what was your image of pro-life people and the pro-life movement?

Well, Father I really didn't know of . . . I didn't know that there was two sides to the abortion issue. I didn't attend any of the court proceedings. I didn't. In fact that's why I used the name Jane Roe because I didn't want my own personal name to be involved in it, because I had always been involved with stuff and it always turned out pretty bad, and I always felt really bad about that. So I wasn't taking a chance with this.

Could you tell us what your position is right now about abortion and the morality of abortion?

Well, the morality of abortion is, it's totally wrong. Since August 8, 1995, I have been pro-life clear across the board.

Now, when you say clear across the board, what do you mean?

Well, I mean I have said in an interview with Ted Koppel back in 1995 that I was still pro-choice, I was still not pro-choice but in favor of a woman's abortion in the first trimester. But then I looked at a fetal development chart at the Operation Rescue Office in Dallas. I had a lot of emotions stirring up inside of me and that's when I decided that it was wrong in any stage of pregnancy.

At any stage of pregnancy and also for any reason?

Absolutely, Father.

Norma McCorvey (center), also known as Jane Roe in the Roe v. Wade *case, leads a demonstration on Capitol Hill in Washington, DC. McCorvey has since reversed her position on abortion, becoming an outspoken advocate for the pro-life movement.* © AP Images/Manuel Balce Ceneta.

Okay, so you would not think, for example, that there could be some circumstances in which it would be all right for a woman to have an abortion?

No, sir.

How did your position on this change?

Well, I had already been attacking, if you could use that word, in a gentle way, the abortionist that I worked for. He's a very greedy man, a selfish man. And we would have patients that would come in and say, Well, I found out, I had all these tests and I found out that my baby is going to have a cleft palate. I'm going like, that's not a reason. That's just an excuse. And the doctor would do the abortion, he would do and charge women money and not even do an abortion. He would lie to them and tell them that they were pregnant. So, seeing him and watching him every Thursday through Saturday do the abortions, making the appointments, for not good reasons. I mean, of course, I don't think there is a good reason for an abortion, but Dr. Jasper made me really realize that it was just a racket. You know, he was just doing it for the money. He didn't care about the women, he didn't care if they got their two week checkups. You know, he didn't care if they had their medications. You know, I mean he never told them you know, like when you have to get this, and this, and this. And it's essential that you take it. He didn't care.

Now that you've become pro-life and you no longer work for him or for the abortion industry, tell us what you do do.

(Laughter) I'm the computer operator for Operation Rescue National. (Laughter)

That's quite an irony, isn't it?

Yes, sir, it is.

And, how about your relationship with the Lord? Has the Lord forgiven you for the past?

Oh yes, He's been very, He's showed me, He has showed me great mercy, great forgiveness and when Rev. Flip [Benham] baptized me last summer in that pool in North Garland, all my sins, regardless of what they were or when I did them were forgiven, and I was washed by the Blood of the Lamb.

Tell us what reaction you've had from the pro-choice community to your conversion.

Oh, they say that I never had any credibility with them. One particular organization, TARAL, said that they used to send me on lecture tours. And I'll go up, I don't even know where your office is. I mean you know that they're based in Austin, TX. So they just made it, they've just done the same thing that they did for me for all the years that I was out. They just tried to discredit me. And it's like I used to tell them often. You know, this is not the right thing to do, you know, there's too many wonderful people out there who can't have children, who would want to have these children. And I gave two of my babies away. There's no excuse for it. But they went to loving parents and that's what counts.

Your children?

Yes. My children.

Some people say, many people say, in fact, that if this conversion to a pro-life commitment happened to you, it can happen to anybody. Is there hope for those who seem to be so hardened in their pro-choice views?

Absolutely, Father. There's a feminist writer by the name of Naomi Wolf who is reconsidering her position on abortion. There's another woman, I can't bring up her name right this minute, who's also reconsidering her position on abortion. So, I mean I think it's just a sign of the times that women are actually seeing for the first time what a depressing and what a holocaust this is to the unborn.

How do we approach those who do have a pro-abortion position to try to get them to convert?

I think with love and understanding. And telling them about Jesus and letting them realize for themselves that the holocaust against the unborn is the greatest sin that they could ever do or even ever participate in.

I'd like to ask you a couple of final questions about what you think people across America should do to help stop abortion, and I'd like if you could address that in a general way and then say specifically to young people, and then specifically to the clergy, and then to those who consider themselves pro-choice. First, in general, what can we do to stop abortion?

I think that every man, woman, and child who believe in God and believe in Jesus—and it doesn't make any difference what religion you are, or how young you are or how old you are—I think if they get up and go to these abortion mills, and stand there—and they don't have to do anything, they can just stand there and pray, I think that would make a lot of difference. We have to be seen in numbers.

To young people, I would say, please listen to your parents. Do not have extra-marital relationships, before you're married. It is a wrong thing to do. God does not like it. It's in the Ten Commandments and we do live by His Book. And that's the best way to start out a marriage is to have both of you to be wholesome.

Now, you are the woman whose name is used to promote this doctrine of choice. What if young people are told by their friends this is my choice you can't tell me what to do. What do you have to say to that?

What I have to say to those young people is that we live in a society today where these children can be wanted children. And even if you don't want to keep this child, after you've had it, there's plenty of young couples out there, there's plenty of young couples everywhere that want children. And, it's not your body, it's not your choice, because you got that from God. He gave that to you and He gave that to you from your Mama and your Daddy.

| "We have fewer rights now than we did
20 years ago. It's getting harder and
harder for women to get abortions."

A Doctor Who Performs Abortions Reflects on Her Experience

Personal Narrative

Susan Wicklund, interviewed by Eryn Loeb

In the following viewpoint, a journalist interviews a doctor who provides abortions. The doctor says she was trained to provide abortions because she believes that doctors who work in reproductive health must meet the needs of all their patients, arguing that abortion is a simple procedure and incredibly common. She contends that the issue of abortion does not belong in the political sphere, because it is the right of every woman to make her own personal decisions about reproduction. Susan Wicklund is a doctor and author of This Common Secret: My Journey as an Abortion Doctor.

Susan Wicklund, interviewed by Eryn Loeb, "The Abortion Doctor," *Salon*, 2008. Copyright © 2008 by Salon. This article first appeared in Salon.com, at http://www.Salon.com. An on-line version remains in the Salon archives. Reprinted with permission. All rights reserved.

Thirty-five years after *Roe v. Wade* [1973] made abortion legal, it is the most common minor surgery in the United States, yet 87 percent of U.S. counties are without a provider. Because of the shortage of doctors trained in providing abortions, dedicated physicians often split their time among several locations, in some cases regularly traveling hundreds of miles to perform abortions in clinics that are open only one day every other week.

The Life of an Abortion Provider

Dr. Susan Wicklund is one of them. She has been providing abortion services for 20 years, first quietly skirting regulations as a general practitioner, then putting in 100-hour weeks as the abortion provider for multiple clinics in the Midwest, and later in her very own clinic in rural Montana. Wicklund's new [December 2008] book, *This Common Secret: My Journey as an Abortion Doctor* weaves her personal story with those of many women she has treated over the years. She deftly turns individual stories into indictments of abortion policies she sees as misleading, condescending and unsafe.

Wicklund describes her work as a privilege and an honor. But it's also a job, often a dangerous one. She has donned disguises to get past the protesters who scream and wave signs outside both her home and her medical office. She's worn a bulletproof vest and carried a gun. In some states, Wicklund is required to read abortion patients misleading, politician-penned scripts that refer to an embryo as an "unborn baby" and warn that the procedure can be fatal (with no mention of the fact that wisdom tooth removal is far riskier).

While young celebrities like Nicole Richie and Jamie Lynn Spears beam and pose through their unplanned pregnancies and movies like *Juno*, *Waitress* and *Knocked Up* portray childbirth as clearly the best path, plenty of people are making other choices, ones we don't hear about. *Salon* spoke with Wicklund recently about the complicated landscape of abortion rights.

[Eryn Loeb:] How did you come to do this work?

[Susan Wicklund:] I had been involved in home births, and midwives were being arrested for practicing medicine without a license. It was important to me to learn how to do abortions for my own patients, because as a young woman I'd had an abortion that was not done under very good circumstances. I really felt that care should be much better than the care I'd received. By my own choice, I was trained to do abortions as part of my medical training.

Shortly after that, I got into private practice, and I was told by the practice that I was not allowed to do abortions. I was angry and very frustrated. At the March for Women's Lives in Washington, D.C., in 1989, I really felt a personal call to action. I went back to the Midwest where I was practicing, made some phone calls, and ended up meeting with directors from a number of different clinics and going to work in the clinics as an abortion provider. Some of them were rather remote and underserved, and they were having a very difficult time finding doctors.

The Stigma of Abortion in the United States

Abortion is a "common secret" in that 40 percent of American women have an abortion during their childbearing years, but it's rarely spoken about. Why do you think there's such profound discomfort in talking about this?

In other cultures and other countries—in Europe, for instance—it isn't such a taboo subject. There's also a much freer atmosphere around recognizing or talking about people's individual sexuality. In this country we have sex all around us, on billboards and in advertising. It's so pervasive, and yet for somebody to have a child out of wedlock, in most communities, is still something that people talk about [negatively]. It's an outward sign that they've had sex. If you've had an abortion, obviously it means you've also had sex. The religious right has told us over and over again that it is wrong, and we continue to buckle under that. I don't understand why.

Your book is full of stories about the women you've treated and the different circumstances under which they come to have abortions. Are there some that particularly stand out for you?

It seems like not a single day goes by without a patient who has an absolutely horrendous situation at home. We had a woman come into the clinic who was abused by her boyfriend, and she was terrified. She felt that if he found out she was pregnant, he would never let her out of his grips. This is a woman who said to me, "If I can't have this abortion, I'll kill myself. But I'm afraid if I do have this abortion, he'll kill me." We don't see situations every day that are so dramatic. But it just drives home how desperate women are. They'll tell me over and over again that if abortion isn't legal, they're still going to end the pregnancy somehow, and if they can't end the pregnancy, they'll end their own life.

We also had a woman recently who was 52 years old and hadn't had a menstrual cycle for over six months. She'd been having peri-menopausal symptoms for two years. Her doctor told her she was in menopause and there was no way she could conceive, and she and her husband hadn't been using birth control because of that. But she did conceive. And she was devastated. This is a woman who had never thought abortion was a good option for women, but she found herself pregnant and was not in a position to carry a pregnancy full term. She was one of the patients we spent a lot of time with, just talking.

There is no typical patient situation. It isn't all students who want to stay in school, it isn't all career women who want to continue with their careers and not have children right now. It isn't all single women who aren't married and not ready to have a child on their own. And it isn't all married women who had kids

but now feel financially strapped. It's all of those women. When people start stereotyping who it is that has an abortion, it drives me crazy.

Working in the Reproductive Health Field

When you work in the area of women's reproductive health, how important is activism?

To me, it's very important that all the people who are working in the clinics are doing it because of their strong belief that women must have freedom of choice. Anyone who comes to those organizations or clinics simply because it's a job treats it very differently and treats women very differently. The clinics that were first opened in the mid-'70s, right after *Roe v. Wade*, were run by people who had very strong feminist backgrounds, and who really knew from experience—possibly their own experience—that women should be treated with care, with dignity, with respect. This was not just [about] coming in for a Pap smear or for contraceptives.

At one of the clinics where I worked, there was a very young woman who was short the amount of money needed for the abortion. She'd come a long distance. It was her second trip to the clinic. The first time she wasn't really sure of her decision. The second time she came back she was very sure of her decision, but she didn't have quite enough money to pay for it. So the clinic sent her away. I went out into the parking lot and talked to her and offered to lend her the money—only because I'd been in that kind of situation myself, and I knew how frustrating it was. I ended up lending her some money so that she could have the procedure done. But I was reprimanded by the administration of that clinic for helping the patient with the funds. I didn't think that was right. It was our job as a clinic to take care of that patient. (There are many facilities—the bulk of clinics—that don't turn patients away, so I don't want people to get the idea that this is a common thing.)

I'm challenged frequently to separate myself, and I'm not good at it. I get very involved in the needs of the patients beyond just their needs at that moment. For instance, making sure that somebody who I worry is a battered woman, or is in need of mental health care, has resources in her hands before she leaves the clinic. Sometimes I'll take their phone numbers home with me and call them a week later to see how they're doing, or if they've gotten the help they need.

Does it take a particular kind of person to do this type of work? There's the immense stress and crazy hours involved, but it's also necessary to really love what you do rather than just feeling obligated to do it.

I have, quite frankly, had physicians I was training to do abortions, and I knew they just didn't have the personality. And I told them that. The majority of physicians who are providing abortions now are my age and older, in our 50s and 60s. Many of them are motivated to do this because they saw women dying from illegal abortions when they were in their residency programs. They're motivated to provide safe abortions because they know that women don't stop having abortions just because it's illegal. They'll still seek them out, but there will be a lot of women who will become infertile or die.

The problem now is to try to find young physicians who understand that abortion care should be part of their entire practice. It shouldn't be that they just do deliveries or just do family practice. Physicians in those specialties need to take care of *all* their patient needs. What if a woman comes in, and you've delivered two of her babies, and she has early breast cancer? She needs to have radiation therapy, but she's also eight weeks pregnant, and she cannot have that treatment unless she has an abortion. If she chooses to have the abortion, that will increase the chances that she's going to live to take care of her two younger children; then you have to send her to a clinic 200 miles away because you won't do the abortion in your office.

It's the most common minor surgery in the United States, but the doctor may not be trained, even though it's a very simple procedure. Or your practice won't allow you to do it, maybe because they don't want the perceived repercussions from the community. So that's what needs to change: Instead of making it an isolated event in an outlying clinic, which may be hundreds of miles away—which is true in most of the rural United States—a woman should be taken care of by her physician, who has been taking care of her for everything else.

The Political Climate Surrounding Abortion

What was the turning point that made you decide to take defensive measures like wearing a bulletproof vest?

When Dr. [David] Gunn was killed [in Florida in 1993], that just changed everything. He was killed the same month that I was getting all these letters from Michael Ross [an antiabortion extremist who was eventually found guilty of intimidation after sending Wicklund more than sixty threatening letters], telling me he was going to tear me limb from limb and kill me. It was complete tunnel vision. I could not think about anything else outside that part of my life.

When I wear a vest or carry a gun, it often strikes me as I pull up to the clinic that this is absolutely absurd. I, as a physician in the United States of America performing a legal procedure, have to go to these measures to make it possible for me to go to work.

We're hearing less about clinic violence, but it's still happening. Last month [December 2007], a clinic in New Mexico was burned to the ground, and two more were attacked. And we don't hear about it on the news. In Denver, protesters are going to the homes of construction workers to try to encourage them not to work on building the [new Planned Parenthood] clinic.

I wonder how easy it is to change people's minds about abortion amid so much rhetoric and so much emotion. How hopeful are you that people can come to understandings on this issue?

I'm actually much more hopeful than I've ever been. And that's because of what I've seen happening with this book. There's a certain number of people who are adamantly antiabortion and will never change their minds. But there's a huge group of people sitting on the fence who have always thought they're antiabortion, but they don't really know why they think that way. Maybe their parents [influenced them], or their church did. But they don't believe they've had a personal experience with it. They don't believe they've ever known anyone who has had an abortion.

I've had people contact me and say, "I always believed I was against abortion. And I read your book, and I really had no idea. I did not understand what it's all about, I did not understand who the women really are, and how personal this is, what the government is doing." One of them was a very good friend of mine, a woman who has heard me before. But when she read the book front to back she called me up and was just sobbing and said, "I get it now. I finally understand what you've been talking about all these years."

You write about how legal and political distractions take up a huge amount of time in your work. In an election year, is there a way you'd like to see the discussion on abortion and reproductive rights framed?

In my opinion, a candidate should get up and say, "Politics has absolutely no business in reproductive rights." A politician should say, "This is not even something I'm willing to discuss. It is a woman's right. It's not my decision." Unfortunately, that's not the way it's happening.

It has been suggested that debate moderators and the media should ask candidates about their position on birth control as a way of getting them to talk about reproductive rights more broadly. Would that be effective?

If we start engaging in that discussion, it becomes, What birth control is OK and what isn't? How far in a pregnancy can you go? Does a woman get to have an abortion if she is raped, or if she is not married? All these circumstances should be taken out of politics completely and out of the discussion.

If they're going to have any discussion in politics, then they need to go right to [saying], "If *Roe v. Wade* is overturned, how long will a woman spend in jail?" Then people back up and say, "Wait a minute, we're not talking about putting women in jail." Well, yes you are. If it's illegal, and a woman has an abortion, she goes to jail. When you start looking at it in those terms, people get more uncomfortable. It's ridiculous to just say it should be illegal and then not talk about what the consequences are.

Dr. Susan Wicklund (left) attends a NARAL Pro-Choice America reception in California. Wicklund has been providing abortions for women for more than twenty years, sometimes traveling in disguise and with a bulletproof vest. © Jordin Althaus/WireImage/Getty Images.

The Change in Abortion Rights

How has the landscape of abortion rights changed over the 20-some years you've worked in this area?

I'm very fearful that we're going to lose *Roe v. Wade*. It's becoming more of a polarized issue all the time. We have the Republicans very adamantly saying we should outlaw all abortion, but the Democrats are also so far to the right on this issue, saying things like "abortion should be extremely rare." It's *not* rare. It's 40 percent of women in this country. And that needs to be acknowledged first.

We have fewer rights now than we did 20 years ago. It's getting harder and harder for women to get abortions. Even if *Roe* doesn't fall, we're still losing providers, we're still losing clinics; there are still laws being passed that are making it more difficult for women, and for the clinics themselves.

Do you think the prominence of young, pregnant celebrities and movies like Knocked Up *and* Juno *have an effect on young women's decisions?*

Is that going to affect the patient from Havre, Mont.? I don't believe it will. The patients I see are so focused on their own lives: a 17-year-old senior who got a full-ride scholarship to a college she's been dreaming of, and her parents have no money, and now she's pregnant. She either stays home and has a baby and probably stays in that town the rest of her life, or she goes off to college and plays basketball. I don't believe that patient's going to care if Britney Spears' younger sister has a baby or not. She's looking at her own life.

On the opposite end, whenever there's more talk about abortion in the media or on TV, I do hear patients mentioning that. I don't hear them mentioning the woman who keeps the pregnancy.

I guess when it's your own experience, it's really set apart from whatever cultural influences are out there.

That is so key. People say they would never have an abortion because of their religion or for whatever other reason. Then they're sitting on that table, we're ready to start doing the abortion, and they want to tell me about how, when they were 17, they made a promise to be abstinent, and here they are at 21, not married and with an unwanted pregnancy. They just want to talk about it and say, I didn't realize—I didn't understand what it would be like when it was me.

Organizations to Contact

The editors have compiled the following list of organizations con-
cerned with the issues debated in this book. The descriptions are
derived from materials provided by the organizations. All have
publications or information available for interested readers. The
list was compiled on the date of publication of the present volume;
the information provided here may change. Be aware that many
organizations take several weeks or longer to respond to inquiries,
so allow as much time as possible.

Advocates for Youth
2000 M Street NW, Suite 750
Washington, DC 20036
(202) 419-3420 • fax: (202) 419-1448
website: www.advocatesforyouth.org

Advocates for Youth is an organization that works both in the
United States and in developing countries with a focus on adolescent reproductive and sexual health. Advocates for Youth
champions efforts that help young people make informed and
responsible decisions about their reproductive and sexual health.
Advocates for Youth publishes numerous informational essays
available on its website, including "Emergency Contraception: A
Safe & Effective Contraceptive Option for Teens."

American Center for Law and Justice (ACLJ)
PO Box 90555
Washington, DC 20090-0555
(800) 296-4529
website: www.aclj.org

The American Center for Law and Justice is dedicated to protecting religious and constitutional freedoms. ACLJ has participated

in numerous cases before the US Supreme Court, the federal Court of Appeals, federal district courts, and various state courts regarding freedom of religion and freedom of speech. ACLJ has numerous memos and position papers available on its website, including "Federal Healthcare Funding and Abortion."

American Civil Liberties Union (ACLU)

125 Broad Street, 18th Floor
New York, NY 10004
(212) 549-2500
e-mail: infoaclu@aclu.org
website: www.aclu.org

The American Civil Liberties Union is a national organization that works to defend Americans' civil rights as guaranteed in the US Constitution. The ACLU works in courts, legislatures, and communities to defend First Amendment rights, the right to equal protection, the right to due process, and the right to privacy. The ACLU publishes the semiannual newsletter *Civil Liberties Alert* as well as briefing papers, including "The Right to Choose: A Fundamental Liberty."

Center for Reproductive Rights

120 Wall Street
New York, NY 10005
(917) 637-3600 • fax: (917) 637-3666
e-mail: info@reprorights.org
website: www.reproductiverights.org

The Center for Reproductive Rights is a global legal advocacy organization dedicated to reproductive rights. The Center for Reproductive Rights uses the law to advance reproductive free-dom as a fundamental human right that all governments are legally obligated to protect, respect, and fulfill. The Center for Reproductive Rights publishes articles, reports, and briefing pa-pers such as the article "Parental Involvement Laws."

Concerned Women for America (CWA)
1015 15th Street NW, Suite 1100
Washington, DC 20005
(202) 488-7000 • fax: (202) 488-0806
website: www.cwfa.org

Concerned Women for America is a public policy women's organization that has the goal of bringing biblical principles into all levels of public policy. CWA focuses on promoting biblical values on six core issues—family, sanctity of human life, education, pornography, religious liberty, and national sovereignty—through prayer, education, and social influence. Among the organization's brochures, fact sheets, and articles available on its website is "It's Time to Reject *Roe v. Wade* as Invincible Precedent."

Guttmacher Institute
125 Maiden Lane, 7th Floor
New York, NY 10038
(212) 248-1111 • fax: (212) 248-1951
website: www.guttmacher.org

The Guttmacher Institute works to advance sexual and reproductive health worldwide through an interrelated program of social science research, public education, and policy analysis. The Guttmacher Institute collects and analyzes scientific evidence to make a difference in policies, programs, and medical practice. The institute's monthly *State Policies in Brief* provides information on legislative and judicial actions affecting reproductive health, such as the recent brief "An Overview of Minors' Consent Laws."

Human Life Foundation, Inc.
353 Lexington Avenue, Suite 802
New York, NY 10016
website: www.humanlifereview.com

The Human Life Foundation, Inc., is a nonprofit organization that works to promote alternatives to abortion through educational and charitable means. The foundation publishes *The Human Life Review*, a quarterly journal that focuses on abortion and other life issues.

NARAL Pro-Choice America

1156 15th Street NW, Suite 700
Washington, DC 20005
(202) 973-3000 • fax: (202) 973-3096
website: www.naral.org

NARAL Pro-Choice America advocates for privacy and a woman's right to choose. NARAL Pro-Choice America works to elect pro-choice candidates, lobbies US Congress to protect reproductive rights, and monitors state and federal activity in the courts related to reproductive rights. NARAL Pro-Choice America publishes numerous fact sheets, including "The Difference Between Emergency Contraception and Early Abortion Options."

National Right to Life Committee (NRLC)

512 10th Street NW
Washington, DC 20004
(202) 626-8800
e-mail: nrlc@nrlc.org
website: www.nrlc.org

The National Right to Life Committee was established to repeal the right to abortion after the decision in *Roe v. Wade* (1973). The NRLC works toward legislative reform at the national level to restrict abortion. NRLC publishes a monthly newspaper, the *National Right to Life News*, and several fact sheets, such as "Teens and Abortion: Why Parents Should Know."

National Youth Rights Association (NYRA)

1101 15th Street NW, Suite 200
Washington, DC 20005

(202) 835-1739

website: www.youthrights.org

NYRA is a youth-led national nonprofit organization dedicated to fighting for the civil rights and liberties of young people. NYRA has more than seven thousand members representing all fifty states. It seeks to lower the voting age, lower the drinking age, repeal curfew laws, and protect student rights.

Planned Parenthood Federation of America

434 West 33rd Street

New York, NY 10001

(212) 541-7800 • fax: (212) 245-1845

website: www.plannedparenthood.org

Planned Parenthood is a sexual and reproductive health care provider and advocate. Planned Parenthood works to improve women's health and safety, prevent unintended pregnancies, and advance the right and ability of individuals and families to make informed and responsible choices. On its website, Planned Parenthood offers information about birth control as well as position papers such as "Affordable Birth Control and Other Preventative Care."

For Further Reading

Books

Scott Ainsworth and Thad E. Hall, *Abortion Politics in Congress: Strategic Incrementalism and Policy Change.* New York: Cambridge University Press, 2011.

Howard Ball, *The Supreme Court in the Intimate Lives of Americans: Birth, Sex, Marriage, Childrearing, and Death.* New York: New York University Press, 2002.

Francis J. Beckwith, *Defending Life: A Moral and Legal Case Against Abortion Choice.* New York: Cambridge University Press, 2007.

David J. Garrow, *Liberty and Sexuality: The Right to Privacy and the Making of Roe v. Wade.* Berkeley: University of California Press, 1998.

N.E.H. Hull and Peter Charles Hoffer, *Roe v. Wade: The Abortion Rights Controversy in American History.* Lawrence: University Press of Kansas, 2010.

Carole Joffe, *Dispatches from the Abortion Wars: The Costs of Fanaticism to Doctors, Patients, and the Rest of Us.* Boston: Beacon Press, 2009.

Christopher Kaczor, *The Ethics of Abortion: Women's Rights, Human Life, and the Question of Justice.* New York: Routledge, 2011.

Paul Benjamin Linton, *Abortion Under State Constitutions: A State-by-State Analysis.* Durham, NC: Carolina Academic Press, 2008.

Catriona Macleod, *Adolescence, Pregnancy, and Abortion: Constructing a Threat of Degeneration.* New York: Routledge, 2010.

Jon L. Mills, *Privacy: The Lost Right.* New York: Oxford University Press, 2008.

Janet E. Smith, *The Right to Privacy.* San Francisco: Ignatius Press, 2008.

Bonnie Steinbock, *Life Before Birth: The Moral and Legal Status of Embryos and Fetuses.* New York: Oxford University Press, 2011.

Periodicals and Internet Sources

Daniel Allott, "Does Roe Still Matter?," *American Spectator,* January 25, 2012. www.spectator.org.

Nancy Belden, "On Solid Ground: Over 35 Years, Abortion Polls Show Remarkable Consistency," *Conscience,* Spring 2008.

Caitlin Borgmann, "Abortion Parental Notice Laws: Irrational, Unnecessary and Downright Dangerous," *Jurist,* July 27, 2009. jurist.law.pitt.edu.

Maggie Datiles, "Parental Involvement Laws for Abortion: Protecting Both Minors and Their Parents," Culture of Life Foundation, April 18, 2008. www.culture-of-life.org.

Steve Dennis, "Liberalism, Replacing Parental Rights with Government Control," AmericasWatchtower.com, October 17, 2007.

Dinesh D'Souza, "Sex, Lies, and Abortion: It's Time to Get to the Bottom of the Great National Tragedy," *Christianity Today,* September 2009.

Family Planning & Contraceptive Research, "A Shifting Landscape: Parental Involvement Laws and Their Effect on Minors," University of Chicago Medical Center, January 13, 2010. www.chicagofamilyplanning.org.

Nancy Gibbs, "Birth Control for Kids?," *Time,* October 18, 2007.

Rachel Benson Gold, "All That's Old Is New Again: The Long Campaign to Persuade Women to Forego Abortion," *Guttmacher Policy Review,* Spring 2009.

Edmund C. Hurlbutt, "Abortion 'Rights' and the Duty Not to Know," *Human Life Review,* Summer 2011.

Deborah Kotz, "Should the Government Pay for Abortions?," *US News & World Report,* December 8, 2008.

Scott Lemieux, "Bypassing Young Women's Abortion Rights," *American Prospect,* August 17, 2007.

Amanda Marcotte, "Conservative Groups Demand High Abortion, Teen Pregnancy Rates," *Slate,* July 13, 2010. www .slate.com.

Ruth Marcus, "Abortion's New Battleground," *Newsweek,* December 7, 2009.

Daniel Patrick Moloney, "Planned Teen Parenthood," *National Review,* July 1, 2008. www.nationalreview.com.

Steven C. Moore, "A Tragic Inheritance: A Personal Perspective on the Abortion Debate," *America,* February 16, 2009. www .americamagazine.org.

Michael J. New, "A Parental-Involvement Opportunity," *National Review,* September 16, 2008. www.nationalreview .com.

Jon O'Brien, "Reducing the Need for Abortion: Honest Effort or Ideological Dodge?," *Conscience,* Spring 2009.

Star Parker and Gary Bauer, "A Dream Unfulfilled: *Roe v. Wade* Has Played a Big Role in the Devastation of the African-American Community," *Weekly Standard,* January 21, 2009.

Jennifer Senior, "The Abortion Distortion: Just How Pro-Choice Is America, Really?," *New York,* December 7, 2009.

Wesley J. Smith, "Abortion Now More Important than Parental Rights," *First Things,* March 24, 2010. www.firstthings.com.

Scott Spear and Abigail English, "Protecting Confidentiality to Safeguard Adolescents' Health: Finding Common Ground," *Contraception*, August 2007.

Michael E. Telzrow, "Before *Roe v. Wade*," *New American*, January 21, 2008.

David Van Biema, "America Without *Roe v. Wade*," *Time*, September 25, 2008.

Index